WINNING
Despite All Odds

WINNING Despite All Odds

Gaurav Krishna Bansal

Ocean Paperbacks
A Division of Ocean Books Pvt. Ltd.
ISO 9001:2008 Publishers

Published by
Ocean Paperbacks
A Division of Ocean Books Pvt. Ltd.
4/19 Asaf Ali Road,
New Delhi-110 002 (INDIA)

ISBN 978-81-8430-121-2
Winning Despite All Odds
by **Gaurav Krishna Bansal**

Edition
2012

Price
Rs. 125.00 (Rs. One Hundred Twenty Five only)

Printed at
Bhanu Printers, Delhi

To

My Parents Shri K.K. Bansal and
Dr. Mrs. Veena Bansal
My Brother Shri Vikas Krishna Bansal and
Bhabhi Smt Rekha V. Bansal
My Wife Swati
My Dad in Law and Mom in Law
Shri Aadarsh Agrawal and Smt. Anita Agrawal
My Brothers in Law Shri Ankit Agrawal
and
Shri Sanchit Agrawal
My Dear *Sahlej,* Monika Agrawal
My Teachers, Seniors and Students
My Wonderful Colleagues and
Staff in Indian Railways
And
My Daughter Gauri, whose hugs and
kisses keep me going!

ACKNOWLEDGEMENTS

I must begin by thanking all the students who inspired me to write this book. I have been delivering motivational speeches to students of Lucknow. I found that the students I addressed were always very receptive and posed relevant and challenging questions. Their feedback convinced me that apart from academic input, guidance and motivation are essential for the success of any individual. It was this realization that spurred me to write 'Despite All Odds'.

Writing is time consuming. Most of my time is taken up by the demands of my official duties and responsibilities. The time that remains belongs to my family,more specifically to my wife and daughter. I have to admit that often I have cannibalized on their share of time in order to produce this work. I am eternally grateful to both of them for allowing me this luxury and especially to my wife Swati for feeding me even when I refused to take her out for a holiday and concentrated on writing instead!

Everything that I am today is due to the untiring efforts of my parents. They have always encouraged me in my literary efforts and have given me the best education and upbringing that any boy could possibly get. Often they have economized on their requirements in order to fulfill mine. It is impossible to thank them in words. However, I still wish to thank them for all they have done and are still doing for me. In the same breath I would like to thank my elder brother Shri Vikas Krishna Bansal. He is a rock around which I can safely tether my ship whenever I return to the shore after a voyage in the sea of this world. My father in law, Shri Aadarsh Agarwal is an amazing man. I wish I had his kind of energy and temperament. I wish to thank him and my mother in law Smt. Anita Agarwal, for always taking pride in my achievements and enjoying them as if they were their own.

Several institutions and organizations have often invited me to address their students and teachers. I wish to thank all of them for having faith in me and my ability to inspire their teachers and staff.

I have relied heavily on the internet during my research for the nations and biographies section of this book. I wish to thank all the URLs and the websites which are so generous in sharing information. I would like to thank the Wikipedia foundation in particular. They are doing a fantastic job. My congratulations to them for their efforts at making quality information available to all!

I thank Shri Roshan Premyogi for always being a friend and a critic.

Last but not the least I wish to thank my colleagues and friends in the Indian Railways. I would like to thank, in particular, Smt Tripti Gurha, for always believing in me, Shri Abhijeet Narendra and Shri Manoj Srivastava for their affection and moral support, Shri BMS Bisht, for incessant encouragement, Shri P K Goel, for giving me a chance when I most needed it, and Smt. Ashima Singh for being not a boss but a mother figure to all of us at IRITM and to me in particular. My thanks to all the staff members of the great Indian Railway family from whom I have received love, affection and support much beyond what I deserve.

❐

INTRODUCTION

At the very outset allow me to quote Charles Dickens. "It was the best of times; it was the worst of times". Perhaps this opening line of his novel 'A Tale of Two Cities', best describes the state of the world that we live in today. It is a strange world, extremely rich and extremely poor, selfish and altruistic, principled and corrupt, advanced and backward, good, bad and ugly, all at the same time. It is a goldmine of opportunity and a quagmire. But the best part is that by and large it is a free world. Barring a few nations of the world where democracy is still a dream and fundamental rights unheard of, the individual in the world of today enjoys unparalleled freedom and opportunity for social, economic and spiritual development. Boundaries of nations are increasingly becoming porous and Information Technology has enabled instantaneous transmission of ideas and knowledge across the globe. Back home, in India, we are witnessing a renaissance of sorts. Post 1991, the reforms in the Indian economy and the loosening of the administrative controls over the lives of citizens have thrown up an array of opportunities which were unimaginable just over two decades ago. Indians are slowly occupying their rightful place in the firmament of the globe as respected global citizens riding on the achievements of the Indian Diaspora that has contributed immensely to the socio-economic development of world superpowers like the USA and Europe. However, all is not hunky dory. The same reforms that have contributed so much towards making India an incipient economic superpower, has also extracted their cost in terms of the cutthroat competition that a youth in India has to face. It starts with the admission in schools and colleges and in institutions imparting professional training. Innumerable coaching centers have sprung up all over India imparting specialized training to students who wish to gain admission into the IITs, Medical Colleges, IIMs etc. The competition for a place in alternative careers like music, dance and sports has also heated up considerably. A serious malaise of corruption pervades our society and system and the general perception, unfortunately, is that it is impossible to achieve success in the absence of money and contacts. With the age of achievement going down every day, a vast majority of young aspirants are under tremendous pressure to outperform their peers. This pressure, unfortunately, has resulted in some very serious and negative social consequences. One manifestation of this pressure is in the form of the spate of 'teen-suicides' that our country is witnessing every year. There is a spate of suicides after the declaration of the result of every major examination in the country, ranging from high school to competitions for a berth in engineering and medical colleges. What is even more alarming is that we are witnessing suicides not only of students who have failed to clear an exam but also of those who have cleared with respectable grades but have not figured in the top bracket. There is also a general loss of values in the society. Money is being viewed as the be-all and end-all of achievement. The desire to get rich quickly with the help of short-cut methods is being reflected in the much enhanced figures of child delinquency in the country. Add to it the media explosion and the situation becomes even grimmer. I will rate the television as the main culprit. All sorts of programming is reaching our youth unchecked and uncensored. Millions of rupees are being handed out to participants of reality shows in return for performing a few tasks and it has seriously downgraded the value of money in the eyes of our youth. Everybody seems to be searching for a 'get rich very quick' mantra. The old established values of hard work based on a foundation of ethics have undergone serious erosion. Good and enriching literature has suffered and pulp-fiction has become the staple of much of the youth that is still interested in reading. The reading habit on the whole has declined and is being reflected directly in the form of a young generation that knows more about Mc Donald's than it knows about its own freedom movement.

This book is an attempt at countering such tendencies in our youth. I am using the word 'attempt' because no single work or the author of such a work can claim to provide all the answers. But in this book I have tried to address those issues that are common to almost all those who are trying to achieve success in their lives. I have tried to illustrate that there is a certain roadmap to success which is common to all fields. There are certain things that an individual must do, certain choices that he/she must exercise and certain qualities that must be cultivated before success can be achieved. I must add that the discussion in this work is not a figment of my own imagination. The issues that I have discussed are mostly those which were present and discussed in almost every seminar on success that I have conducted to-date. Some of these were discussed with me in private by the participants of the seminars and lectures. In the entire book, the single point that I have relentlessly driven home is the fact that before pointing a finger at someone else, a person must realize that three of his fingers are pointing back towards his own self! No one achieves success without some serious introspection. "Forgive others but never yourself" is the central theme of this work. This book is all about setting personal standards and achieving them. My thesis is that the factors that are most in our control are those related to our own thought-process, word vision, and attitude. Instead of wasting time fretting over things that an individual cannot control, one should rather try to focus on those things that he/she can control. More often than not, it is this kind of work-by one's own self-that brings the hitherto unachievable into the realm of the achievable.

I have divided this book into three parts. The first part discusses issues like getting a basic understanding of the phenomenon of 'success', dealing with challenges like lack of money, lack of coaching, lack of a 'family background', inability to concentrate, getting jilted in love etc. The second part, from which he title of this book originates, illustrates through very concise and pointed parts of the histories of three nations, the USA, Germany and Japan; all three in the backdrop of World War II and through brief biographies of some famous personalities like Abraham Lincoln, Stephen Hawking, Lal Bahadur Shastri, Thomas Alva Edison etc. that show how determined and untiring effort with a 'never say die' attitude can lead a person to greatness despite all odds. The third part of the book, with the sub-title "The Ugly Duckling", is my own story. It is, let me add, not a complete autobiography. Rather it is an illustrative case study of a normal person, in a normal city of India, with a normal upbringing. I have no illusions about my own self and I am, most certainly, not a celebrity. I have included my case study in the book so that a lay reader can appreciate the fact that even the author of this book on success, attitude and motivation did not get everything served on a platter. I am your typical 'guy next door' and I hope that you will be able to relate to my failures and understand that a failure is actually a building block of success. The only capability that is required is the willingness to accept a failure, take responsibility, draw lessons from it and start afresh with the benefit of hindsight.

I hope that you will find in this book, not a book, but a friend. I will be eagerly looking forward to your feedback, comments and criticism.

Hoping to hear from you,

Yours truly,
Gaurav

CONTENTS

WINNING : DESPITE ALL ODDS

I once read a story. It is an old and popular one. In fact, it is so old and so popular that most of us must be aware of it. But just in case you are one of those few who have not read or heard this story, I will repeat it here for your benefit. It is the story of the ugly duckling.

It goes this way. There was once a duck. A big fat, plump and caring mother duck. She had just laid a clutch of eggs and was busy incubating them. In her duckly-thoughts she could already picture her brood of ducklings. She could imagine the little round and yellow balls of fluff that would come out of the eggs. They would cluster around her feet giving baby-duck calls. They would follow her around and take their first webby-feeted steps into the cold water of the lake. They would swim around making her life beautiful. And they would scramble on her back the moment she called. She would indeed be the most proud and happy mother duck in the whole universe. Suddenly her thoughts were broken by a sudden growl in her stomach. "Oh jumpin fish!" She thought. "Time I had something to eat." So she got up, gave herself a good shake and ambled off to the lake to have a bite.

While she was away, a mother swan came strolling along. She had just laid a clutch of eggs and was going to the lake to have a bath. She was snow white, with a red beak and a graceful and slender neck. Even as she walked she invited glances full of admiration from the inhabitants of the lake and the surrounding reeds. Suddenly she had a strange feeling. It was as if another egg was on its way out. She panicked. She could neither stop the egg, nor could she delay its arrival. The only option was to lay the egg in the open where it had no chance of survival. Even if she tried to make a run for her nest she could not hope to reach it in time. Then her glance fell on the mother duck's nest of eggs. She saw a chance for her egg. Rushing to the nest, she laid the egg in it. Then, satisfied that her egg was safe, she walked off.

When the mother duck returned, she had a strange feeling that something was wrong. One of the eggs looked larger. There also appeared to be more eggs than she had left behind. "Croakin frogs" she thought. "I seem to have eaten too much of the shellfish. They always make me sleepy. And now I am so sleepy that I am seeing things. I'd better get back to incubating my eggs before they get cold" And so she settled herself once more on the eggs and went back to her duckly-thoughts.

Days passed by and soon it was time for the eggs to hatch. Just as the mother duck had imagined, little balls of yellow fluff started to come out of the eggs. They were even more beautiful than she had pictured. After all the eggs had hatched, one still remained. It still seemed larger. Then all of a sudden the shell of the last egg began to crack open. A large beak came out followed by a strange ugly head and then out came the entire duckling. Mother duck was shocked to see it. It was decidedly ugly. It was a strange shade of white and was large, ungainly, and awkward. "Wrigglin tadpoles, what happened to this one?" She thought. But she was after all a mother duck. And it's hard to imagine a more loving and caring person than a mother duck. So she loved the ugly duckling regardless of how it looked. But the poor fellow was not happy. He was the butt of jokes of all his siblings. Even the other birds made fun of him. He was friendless and forsaken and utterly miserable. As time passed by he grew more and more depressed with his life. He had still not befriended any duck and his mother was now busy with a new clutch of eggs. This went on, till, one day, he decided that he had had enough. The best way out was to end his worthless life. So he waddled out to the lake and decided to run away to the other bank, where there were foxes and weasels. As he was swimming away to the other bank he heard steady and powerful wing beats. Looking up he saw three beautiful birds flying overhead. They were simply gorgeous. Their feathers were as white as snow and their beaks were a lovely shade of pink. Their jet-black legs were tucked neatly beneath their short tails as they propelled themselves forward with rhythmic and powerful beats of their long and graceful wings. The ugly duckling watched in awe. How he wished that he could be as beautiful as those birds. Paddling slowly he reached the other bank of the lake. The water there was crystal clear. It was because no birds visited that bank for the fear of foxes and weasels. "Fox! Weasel! Come eat me!" he shouted. But not a fox or weasel appeared. Further depressed, he sat down at the bank of the lake and started crying. He was so ugly that even the foxes and weasels did not want to eat him. Large drops of salty tears welled up in his eyes and dropped into the water. The shimmering water caught his attention and, looking down at the water for the first time in his life, he was surprised to find that the beautiful birds he had seen flying over the lake lived inside the water. Then he moved his head and the beautiful bird inside the lake also moved its head. The ugly duckling was surprised. Slowly, the realization dawned on him. It was not another bird beneath the surface of the lake. It was his own reflection. He couldn't believe it. He knew that the birds he had seen were swans. And, staring back from the mirror-like surface of the lake was a beautiful swan. Flapping his powerful wings, the ugly duckling took off into the blue sky to reclaim his rightful place among his own kind as a beautiful swan.

I told the entire story with a purpose. Does it remind you of yourself? Have you ever felt like the ugly duckling of the story? Friendless, forsaken, worthless, depressed and utterly miserable? Have you ever felt as if the best solution to your problems is to end it all in one glorious leap from a high-rise building? My guess is that the answer to these questions must be 'yes' for you as it is for the majority of us. If indeed it is a 'yes' then this book is for you. So go ahead, read it and discover the beautiful swan within yourself.

What is Success?

Do you consider yourself to be unsuccessful? Are you sure that it is definitely not your fault? It's only natural. Success is always our own doing and failure is always attributed to so many reasons, all of them way beyond our control. The situation, however, is not so simple. Of course you worked. You worked really hard. Blood grime and sweat–the works so to say. But you still ended up a failure? Right? Well, I don't deny that you did work. But maybe you missed the crucial point. So before we look any further we will have to look at that point.

Mull on this for a moment: "Success is a decision"

Sounds strange? Does it? How can success be a decision? It is a consequence not a decision. Success is what you get as a result of a lot of hard work. It's a chance. You cannot say that–I have decided that I am a successful person. No matter how hard you work, success may or may not come.

Fair enough. That is after all the thought process of a majority of us. But think again. Let's say that you were going on a holiday trip. What would you do? Would you pack your bags, buy the ticket, make reservations in hotels, book your taxis, and then finally decide where you'd want to vacation? Obviously not. The order is wrong. First you would spend a great deal of time on deciding where you want to go and then you'd book the tickets, make reservations, book taxis and finally pack your bags. Common sense you would say. But it is this common sense that most of us forget to use when setting out on the most crucial journey of our lives, the road to success.

Now let us go back to the original assertion. "Success is a decision." You are never successful till you decide to be successful. Again, you cannot decide to be successful till you are clear about your definition of success. To be very exact, every person's definition of success is different from that of others. I would say that it is as unique as a fingerprint. So many of us make the mistake of confusing our success with the perception that others hold for us. We use the benchmarks of others as a measure of our own success. Thus, in the process, once again, we miss the whole point. To one person, success could mean a lot of money, to the other, stability, and to still others it could mean adventure, growth, responsibility, fame, love, job satisfaction, or all of these in various combinations. Most of us make the mistake of ordering what the other person orders in a restaurant and finding it unpalatable. In other words, it is called jumping into the bandwagon. So think again. Have you made the mistake of ordering a meal you don't relish in the first place? Have you jumped into the bandwagon? Are you desperately trying to prove that you are as good as the company you are in when you don't want to be a part of it in the first place? The answer to all these questions could be a 'yes' a 'don't know' or a 'maybe'. So how do we find the answer to the problem? Maybe this story will help us arrive at a solution:

The unhappy surgeon

There was once a world famous surgeon. He was simply the best. They said that he could make a dead man rise. Not only was he a good surgeon he was also a very good human being and was loved by all who knew him. After a long and illustrious career spanning over five decades, he decided to retire. All his friends, well-wishers and the patients he had served selflessly decided to organise a farewell party for him. It was a magnificent party. The surgeon was overwhelmed. A huge stage was set up and a troupe of dancers was performing on stage. The surgeon sat with his best friend on the front seat watching the show. Suddenly his friend noticed that the surgeon had tears in his eyes.

"What happened Tom?" he asked. He thought that the surgeon was becoming emotional at the love with which he had been showered. Or perhaps he was already missing his work.

"Nothing Mike" replied the surgeon.

"Oh come on Tom. I have never seen tears in your eyes and I have known you for a good thirty years now. You are retiring only because you are too old to operate on your patients. But look how much every one loves you. Besides, you will not be stopping work altogether. Any hospital will welcome you as a consultant surgeon."

The surgeon was quiet. But tears flowed out of his eyes and rolled down his cheeks.

"Come on Tom. Tell me what the matter is. Surely you can confide in your best friend"

"Actually Mike..." began the surgeon. "Actually I am not crying for any of the reasons you have mentioned. I am retiring from work at the pinnacle of my profession. All kinds of awards and recognitions have come my way. I am loved, appreciated and even revered. I am truly blessed"

"Then why the tears Tom?"

"You know Mike, as I sit here and enjoy this magnificent party; I realize that I always wanted to be a dancer. A lot of people would love to be in my place today. But I would be truly happy if I could be in the place of one of the dancers on the stage"

The story hits. Doesn't it? Unfortunately a lot of us could end up as our surgeon in this story. It's the end result of jumping into the bandwagon. Most of us chase mirages like money, stability, growth etc in our climb to success. What we fail to realize is that the real measure of success is not how rich or famous we are but how content and happy. This once again brings me back to the original assertion.

"Success is a decision"

Before you embark on the journey to success you have to decide what success is. You may be just out of secondary school or fresh into college. You may have a myriad array of options before you. Engineering, Medicine, BBA, MBA, BCA, MCA, Civil Services, Law...the list goes on. So what do you do? I have asked a lot of students why they chose the career option that they did. The most frequent replies are as follows:

"Because all my peers chose this option"

"My dad told me so"

"It's the in thing"

"What else?"

Rather vague don't you think? Is it right to commit yourself to a particular career just because all your peers are doing it or because your dad thinks it is right for you or because it is the latest fad, or worst of them all, you simply don't know of anything else? Going back to our vacation analogy, it means that you boarded a plane that everybody else was boarding, or the one your dad told you to board, or because that plane was fancy or simply because you never tried to find out about any other flight. What can be the outcome of such a move? One, the plane crashes because everybody boarded the wrong plane and everybody dies, (you being one of them). Two, the plane does reach the destination but you find the journey awful and the destination even worse. Three, your dad loved his ride but you hate the plane he put you on to. Four, you end up in a strange land wishing that you had done more research before boarding the plane. Five, by sheer luck you find the flight just swell and the destination, the land of your dreams. Of course, there could be a lot more of permutations and combinations of the possible outcomes that I have listed above but still the last outcome would be just one of those several. Finally as we add every extra permutation or combination, our probability of hitting the bull's eye by sheer chance decreases in the same proportion. In such a circumstance, success becomes subject to luck and the laws of probability no matter how hard we work. This is precisely why we end up saying that success is a matter of chance.

Actually attaining success is simple. It is a decision with two rules:

(1) You decide what your definition of success is, i.e. what would make you happy once you have achieved it.

(2) You decide that you will reach there come what may.

The first of the two decisions is the more difficult

one. It is because the proof of the pudding is in its eating. You can never be entirely sure of a particular career till you have experienced it first hand just as you can never be sure of the taste of a pudding till you eat it. But, suppose I were to ask you to select the best pudding for a party. What would you do? Here is what I would do. I would go to the best bakers of the city, take a look at there wares, consult some people with experience of puddings, consider my own taste, reject any shops that appear unhygienic or seedy in the first instance, consider the price, ask for a sample if the store offers one, and then trust my gut instinct while making the final choice. The same goes for a career. Before you commit yourself, you have to first consider your own tastes and inclinations, look for the best, seek competent advice and, in the end, do what your heart tells you to do. Such an approach may make you the butt of jokes in the beginning, you may be labelled a rebel, or even irresponsible but it does not matter. You have to wear the suit in the end. So it is better if it fits you. Don't you think that it is good idea to spend some time and effort trying to get such a suit stitched? I must throw in a word of caution though. Our expectations should have a basis. You can't expect to be an Einstein if you can't add two plus two. You definitely can't be a dancer if you have two left feet and a singer if you can't carry a beat or stick to a scale. However, the general experience is that most of us love doing some or the other activity. All of us have some inborn talents. Some of us can carry a tune better than the others. Others can write better and still others have a better head for figures or can hit a ball better than our peers. Because we are inherently good at some activities, doing them gives us immense pleasure and satisfaction. Such innate superiorities are called 'talent' in general terms and most of our talents express themselves as activities we call hobbies. Once I read a quote which said "True happiness is when your hobby becomes a means of livelihood"

Now just mull over this statement for a moment. Wouldn't it be great to get paid for an activity that you would do for free? Imagine the output in such a scenario. You could be at the top in no time. And once you are there you could savour the happiness of being there.

So the message is simple. Don't rush. Only fools jump to conclusions before arriving at them. Take your time. Do your research. Evaluate your self. If necessary, get yourself evaluated by a professional. Talk to people in different careers. Ask them for their honest and objective opinion. Ask them if they have enjoyed or are enjoying their journey. Gather information from as many sources as you can. Introspect. See which career you find most appealing after all the research work and then make a decision.

The importance of making this decision cannot be overstressed. Once the decision has been made, you have chosen your destination. The direction is decided. And success, let me stress, is a vector quantity. Those of us who remember some of our high-school physics will recall that a vector quantity has both magnitude and direction. Success is vector because no magnitude of work will get you success till your direction is firmly established. Ideally, the direction should be 100% precise. But that is not usually possible. All the measures that I have outlined above will not only help you to decide your destination (direction) but will also help you to set the shortest and the most efficient route towards it so that the same magnitude of work gets you that much closer to your goal. You must have wondered why some people manage to achieve so much more than you even when they appear to work so much less. The answer is in front of you now. Such people are well directed. They are able to get the maximum output from their efforts because they put it in the right place in the first go. They are people who have taken the decision. Consequently, they appear contented, efficient and in control. Do you want to join the ranks of such people? Go ahead. Take the decision!

Let us now come to the second decision. Assuming that you have already decided where you want to go on vacation, you have to ***want*** to get there. You can't say that I will take that vacation after a month. After a month, it may be too late. The rains may set in. Your boss may refuse to give you leave. Some emergency may crop up that may prevent you from asking for leave in the first place. Finances may go downhill. The flights may be all booked. Civil unrest may surface at a place that was heaven only a month ago. Government of that place may change and impose a ban on the entry of outsiders.... The possibilities are endless. The net outcome is the same. You may end up missing the vacation completely. Time is of essence. Once your decision of reaching a particular destination has been taken, all other destinations should be blocked out till you reach that one. All efforts must be started immediately. Nose to the grindstone is the rule. Dilly-dallying is a strict no-no. Now that you know where you have to go, rest is formality and will power. Everything else can wait. You have to want to get there. It has to be in your system. If it requires study, then you have to do so without your parents chiding you for it. If it is art or sport, you have to practice without anybody telling you to do so. It has to come from within. You have to be a self-starting engine rather than a kick-starting one. All options have to be explored. The thrust has to be towards reaching the destination in the shortest possible time. Effort must not be a consideration. Remember, you have decided. You are committed. No decision is a decision unless enforced. No commitment is a commitment unless kept. Once this decision is made, the term 'if' in your vocabulary should be replaced by 'when'. Once the decision to be successful has been taken, you will no longer say, "If I become…." In its place you will start saying "when I become…". Let me tell you. It is not easy to substitute 'if' with 'when'. Most of us are brought up to believe that success is a chance. It is a possibility but never a certainty. However, as soon as you start using 'when' in place of 'if' success becomes a certainty. It's a paradigm shift. With the substitution of a single word, established dogmas are broken. A new light emerges. You feel more confident, more in control and one hundred per cent committed. Your goal comes clearly into your sights. You become completely focused. You are no longer apologetic about your goal. You are no longer afraid to announce it to all and sundry from rooftops. You are no longer afraid of failure. Failure is no longer an option. Reaching your goal is a certainty. It's no longer a question of "if you reach there" it is only a matter of "when you reach there".

Lack of a suitable background

In my sessions with students, this is the most frequently asked question. Most of us feel that we don't have the background or the upbringing to achieve our goals. Glaring examples around us reinforce this belief. We see sons and daughters of top actors becoming successful actors after getting dream-breaks. We see wards of successful politicians getting elected to the parliament almost unopposed. We see ofsprings of successful doctors and lawyers inherit the practice of their parents. Consequently, we slip into a depression. We start believing that success is reserved for only a few who were lucky enough to be born in the right homes. If that is the case with you, think again.

Instead of focusing on the second generation, try to focus on the first generation. Somebody from the grassroots rose up to become a successful politician before his son could gain the advantage. The same is the case with successful doctors, lawyers, actors, businessmen, bureaucrats, artists and others. Not everybody gets the advantage of being the second generation. But nobody can be stopped from being the first generation. Remember, there was a first generation to every second or third or fourth generation. Every great dynasty was started by some ordinary man, who believed that he could be a king. Look at history. From the Mauryas, to the Delhi Sultanate to the Mughals, all dynasties have had humble beginnings. They all rose to greatness and then all of them declined. The first generation aspirant has a disadvantage over the second or third generation man in as much as he has to cover a lot of ground merely to get to the starting line of the latter. But he also has an advantage. His achievements are his own. He does not carry the weight of expectations. He does not have to carry forward what his father started. He can choose his own calling. Besides, if, by chance, the second or third generation in the dynasty is heading towards a decline and the people are looking for a change then he has a real chance of filling up the void. It is agreed that it is more difficult for the first generation aspirant to attain success but it is much easier for him to retain it. That is because he knows the ropes from the strings and the nuts from the bolts. The second generation is denied this crucial advantage. They inherit the baggage. Their freedom of choice in terms of friends, advisors and confidants is severely limited. On the other hand the first generation is free to choose. There is no baggage. No limits on choice of resources or partners. The initial climb to the top is undoubtedly tougher because there are a lot of people at the bottom clamouring to go up. But once the initial few rungs of the ladder are below you, the rest of the climb is much faster and smoother. Examples are aplenty. One that I would love to quote is of our former president Dr. APJ Abdul Kalam who sold newspapers on a railway platform as a child. There are many more and I do not wish to produce a list of names. You will find that in every other book on motivation. My point is simple. Lack of background cannot be a reason for failure just as presence of background cannot be a reason for success.

Lack of Coaching and Money

That is the next question that crops up. "I live in such and such place where adequate coaching is not available for my field. I do not have adequate money. My parents are not rich enough to pay the exorbitant fee of the coaching institute. I want to play tennis but we have no courts in the city. I want to be an actor but...." These are the most frequent excuses from students of any discipline. Coaching is the buzzword today. It has been accepted as the panacea for all ills ailing one's career. It is considered to be the key that will open all locks. While I do not deny the importance of a proper coach for the success of any aspirant in his chosen field, the statements reproduced above are nothing more than excuses of half-hearted people. I can begin by giving my own example. I competed in the civil services with Zoology and Botany as my subjects. 1200 out of the 2300 marks in the competition were to be earned in these subjects. When I started preparation there was no coaching in Lucknow that could guide a candidate in these subjects. I did not know which books to read, what to remember, and how to write answers. So, by conventional logic, I should have failed. But I didn't. I decided to tackle the problem head on. I consulted competition-oriented magazines. In one such magazine I came across the interview of Dr. Himani Pandey who had succeeded in the Civil Services Exam with the same subjects and had secured a very good rank. In her interview she had mentioned the titles and authors of the books that she had read as part of her preparation for the competition. I immediately went to my local bookseller and ordered the books that she had listed. Sure enough, once the books arrived I was shocked to find the difference in standard between the books that she had recommended and the ones, which I was reading. I studied from those books and made it through to the written exam. But I did not fare too well in the written and got eliminated in the interview. I was at a loss. I had worked hard, put in my best and yet met failure. Or had I? I decided to look at it differently. Approximately three hundred thousand students had appeared in the competition that year. Out of those only about five thousand had made it through the screening (preliminary exam) to the written (main) exam and of those, around six hundred had received the call for the interview. That meant that I had managed to secure a place among the first six hundred of the country out of three hundred thousand aspirants! Suddenly the feeling of failure was replaced by the smell of success. I decided to go ahead and give it another shot. But before I did that I analysed my mark sheet.

Upon analysis I found that I had secured less than expected marks in all the papers of my subject, but in one paper, which I thought I had written badly, I had secured very good marks. I sat back and took another look at the question paper. I analysed the kind of questions I had chosen and the kind of answers I had written. I found that in that particular paper I had chosen questions with several parts and my answers had been highly diagrammatic. Moreover, I had clearly brought out the structural-functional linkage in animals. That was the key. In the next attempt I maintained the same focus and was selected in all three competitions I appeared in, namely Indian Forest Services, Civil Services and Provincial Civil Services. I had also sought the guidance of my University Professors in the matter. Some had been keen to help, others had not been so keen, but none were reluctant. Their valuable inputs were a great help in improving my scores.

The point that I am trying to make here is that the term 'coaching' has been distorted and made narrow so as to be interpreted as 'class room coaching'. This is fallacy. The fact is that coaching can be of many types. It may be class-oriented or distance learning, continuous or intermittent, lecture-oriented or problem solving type. The challenge is not to find the right 'coaching' but to find the right 'coach'. I have mentioned a few options above. The correct books, magazines, teachers and self-introspection can each serve as a coach to the motivated aspirant. We live an age of advanced information technology. The print, computer and audio- visual aids like television and internet are constantly bombarding us with information. Each of these can be used by the aspirant as a tool for achieving success. The crux is how the aspirant uses them. In today's world, media is a double edged sword. It can make or mar careers depending upon its use.

In the unlikely event that a candidate is so isolated that he or she has no avenues of suitable guidance in his or her native place, the only option is to go where the avenues are. It is beyond doubt that it is difficult and even painful. But then, who said that the road to success is easy? Remember, you are committed. When faced with such a dilemma, consider the following situation.

Imagine that you are in love with someone. You are committed. You can't live without that person. You have to get married to him/her. But everybody is against the marriage. What would you do? Would you simply walk away from the relationship saying that you are unable to keep your commitment because there are too many obstacles in the way? Or would you move mountains to keep your commitment? Chances are that you would do anything and everything in your power including the risking of your life in order to be with the person you truly love. Now just juxtapose this situation to career and success. The answer is obvious. If you let go, you were never committed in the first place. You failed right in the beginning. You never took that important decision. There was doubt when there should have been certainty. You did not want to succeed with all your heart. You were doomed to fail even before you began.

The other side is much different. If you don't let go, then you will make plans to overcome the hurdles. You will search for the nearest location where you can get suitable guidance for your aim, be it study, sport or art. If necessary you will relocate. Lack of finances will not stop you. You will work for a scholarship or a grant. If there is no such scholarship available you will take a loan from a friend or a bank. If that is also not possible, you will work in the evenings and prepare for your goal in the day. You will ration your food, sleep and leisure but you will not allow your goal to suffer. And, in the end you will emerge victorious. Of course it will be painful, and time consuming. Others with better means will make it one year or two years ahead of you. But life is not of one year or two years. In the long run you will be the more suitable candidate. You will have developed the capacity to tackle problems head-on and independently. You will have seen the bottom of the pit and will do everything in your power to avoid falling back. Just as a body-builder comes out of the gruelling sessions in the gymnasium with a perfectly sculpted body, you will have come out of your trials with a perfectly sculpted mind and spirit, ready to tackle whatever challenges life throws your way and well oiled to take advantage of the slightest opportunity.

Nice speech, you may say. Have you done it yourself Mr. Bansal? The answer is no. I was fortunate enough to be born in a home and family where I did not have to face the trials I have listed above. But I had my own share of problems, one of which I have already mentioned. Your problem may be bigger than mine, but it's only a difference of degrees. The fact is that a problem is always a problem. Any problem is insurmountable if left untackled and all problems can be overcome if tackled head-on. The problem is not the problem itself but the attitude towards the problem. Sometimes you may have to travel on a third class train over a fourth-class route in order to get to your chosen vacation-spot. You can't wish away the pain but you can definitely lessen the sensation if you are able to imagine the great time that awaits you when, eventually, you get there.

Possession of resources like background, money, coaching, and the inability to concentrate

This is undoubtedly a difficult situation. I will tackle it from the point of view of a student, but the message is equally applicable to a sports person or an artist. This is precisely the problem that I faced. I was born in a family of bureaucrats and grew up in a good city. I was not unintelligent either. Yet I was a failure. I could not bring myself to concentrate on my studies. I failed repeatedly. I was thrown out of high school for failing to make the grade and successively failed to qualify in competitive entrance examinations for medicine and then law. I was down in the dumps and thought that I would amount to nothing. It was not as if I was not aware of the fact that I needed to work, but I just couldn't bring myself to spend enough time on the study-table. One day, when I was trying to force my self to concentrate on studies, a thought struck me. It was that thought that changed my life. Maybe it will help you too.

You have got parents who are willing to support you financially. You live in a good house in a good city. You have a room all to yourself with its own air-conditioning and phone connection. The facility of laundry and room service is available to you because you have servants to work around the house. You are also lucky enough to possess a car or a bike and enjoy cable television and internet facility in your room. To top it all, you get a monthly allowance from your parents and can even afford having a girlfriend! In short you have a comfortable and happy existence where your time is not subject to the whims and fancies of anyone else and you can choose to use it the way you wish to. Out of the eighteen hours that you usually spend waking, you still can't bring yourself to spend eight on your career. You want to do it but you just can't!

If that is your situation, just take some time off to think on this. Take a piece of paper and jot down the facilities that are available to you for free because dad pays for them. Now try to transform these into monetary terms and arrive at the amount of money needed to support a single person who has all the facilities. In any good Indian city, this figure works out to approximately ten thousand rupees to twelve thousand rupees per month. Now remove dad from the equation. What happens? Suddenly you are on your own. If dad was not there you would have had to earn all this money yourself merely to maintain your present standard of living. Now, suppose you did have to earn the money yourself. How much work would an employer expect from you for this kind of money? I raised the question to a number of students and the lowest figure that I received was a minimum of eight hours per day. Accepting the lowest figure as the standard, let us proceed forward. Now the situation is that you are supporting yourself to your present standard of living and the minimum amount of work that your organization expects you to put in is eight hours per day. Remember, this time could go up depending upon the quantum of work. So, essentially, you have no control over your own time. Thus, in terms of time usage, you have much less flexibility. In addition, there are responsibilities, deadlines and unfinished assignments that occupy your mind even when you are not working. That, in essence, reduces your peace of mind by a large extent. You could exist like this forever, but there is a catch. With your present qualifications you do not see any career growth in future. If you have to climb up the ladder, you will have to squeeze extra time out of your day in order to prepare yourself for that important examination which will get you admitted into that important institute which in turn will lead to a quantum jump in your career. In the absence of dad to support you, so many other chores will have to be done by you and they will place additional demands on your limited time. So you will have to be extra-committed, extra-laborious and extra-efficient if at all you have to amount to anything much in life. Sounds bleak, does it? Of course it does. And I have yet not factored in the occasional illness and the resulting medical bills and problems, the tax returns that you have to file on time, the investments that you have to make for a better tomorrow and the time you have to extract to keep your girlfriend happy. Does it sound much worse now? If it does, just compare your present quality of life with the picture I have painted above. I am sure that it is vastly superior. But will it always be like this? Could have been, but for the bitter truth that dad will not be there forever. There will be one point in time when you will be left alone and will be forced to fend for yourself whether you like it or not. What is the moral of the story? It is obvious, isn't it? There are no free lunches. Whatever you are enjoying today, is paid for. The cost is still being incurred. It's only that ***you*** are not footing the bill. It's a sort of credit that you are taking from dad. It's an opportunity that you are getting. Ten to twelve thousand rupees a month is what your dad spends on you. If it were a salary given by a boss, he would suck you dry in exchange. Dad, being dad, asks for nothing in return. He can't fire you from the job like a boss can. You are, consequently lulled into a false sense of security. It is false because this security is not permanent. One day it will go with dad. That will be the day when the accounting of this time and money will be done by the world at large. That will be the day when you will look back and repent at the wasted time and opportunity both of which are not going to return.

So what do you do? Start maintaining a salary book.

Each month you receive up to twelve thousand rupees worth of facilities as salary and you have to give a minimum of eight hours per day as work in return with one day off each week. Not much is it? After all it is the minimum that any employer would expect. And the bright side is that all this work and time will be invested not in improving the financial health of your employer but in improving your own prospects for the future.

This is the thought that changed my life. I set up my room like an office with a table, chair, bookshelves, table lamp, stationery, visitors' chairs....the works. I imagined that every morning I was reporting to my office at nine am. There was a half an hour lunch break in the afternoon and then work went on till six in the evening. After six, I left office (my room) went out for a short stroll, enjoyed some programmes on the television and then, after dinner, put in an additional hour in order to complete some backlog of work that was required in the office the next day. Targets were fixed and work was project oriented as the time available was finite. Suddenly, concentration was not a problem. As I delved deeper into my work (study), I realised that I had already been left much behind my peers. I had already wasted enough time so as to be at a disadvantage relative to them. I had to put in those extra hours if I had to catch up. I no longer needed the chiding from mom or dad in order to study. In fact, now the situation was the other way round. Now they were asking me to rest. With this regular routine, I was able to balance study and leisure and move unerringly towards my target which I eventually achieved.

You can do the same. It doesn't matter in which field

you are. Give the devil his due. You are getting credit today. You will have to pay tomorrow and that too with interest. There is no better time to prepare for it than now.

The right way to study

How to study? If that is your problem you will be glad to know that there are some rules of the game.

1. **Study is done on a table, not a bed:** A lot of us are in the habit of studying on the bed or on the sofa with music playing and the phone ringing. Now think about it. Study is a kind of work. Most of the managers and professionals do a lot of study in the course of their work. But have you ever seen a doctor, or an engineer or a bureaucrat or any other professional in his or her office working on a bed or sofa. Most likely not. In every office you see neat workstations with a table and a good chair as the principal components. If the best and most successful people in the world are not using a bed as their workstation, it must be for some reason. The reason is simple. A bed is made for rest, not for work. It induces sleep not alertness. It is designed to give you the maximum output from your hours of sleep and not wakefulness. Using a bed or a sofa as a study-station is self destructive. You spend the same amount of time and get little output, if any. If you don't believe me, try switching to a regular study table and a chair for a few days and watch the difference.
2. **Good study is done in silence:** While all of us enjoy music, it is best avoided when doing

serious work. The way our brain is wired, concentration is the most difficult job to accomplish. Add a distracting background score to that and concentration goes for a toss. Most of us lull ourselves into thinking that we concentrate better with a musical score playing in the background. If that were true, then all drivers would be advised to install radio sets and cassette players in their vehicles without fail. In fact it would be made a law. But research shows that music is distracting when you are trying to concentrate on something else. If you love music, set it aside as a treat to be enjoyed after work. Half an hour with good, uninterrupted music of your choice will be more soothing than a day of background music when you are studying. There is another angle also. If you get used to enjoying music while you are solving problems, it becomes a habit. In psychological terms it is called conditioned response. You are able to give the maximum output only when you have music playing in the background. But there is catch. There surely isn't going to be any music in the examination hall. On the contrary there is going to be absolute silence. The essential stimulus that you have become used to will be missing. The result will be a drop in performance, no matter how slight. Thus in a competitive exam where everything hinges on that single question, this drop could prove disastrous. The point is that while studying you must keep the final conditions in mind. An athlete who wants to win a medal in the Olympics tries to train in conditions which are as close to the actual ones as possible. Any tennis player will tell you that there is a world of difference between a grass-court and a clay-court. Similarly, when preparing for the final test, you should be preparing yourself to work in absolute silence rather than in a musical rhapsody.

3. **Effective study is done with a syllabus:** Studying without a syllabus is like driving without a route map. You will end up going around in circles. The best method is to get a photocopy of the syllabus for the exams and keep it at hand at all times. As you complete a topic, you can strike it out from the syllabus. It helps to keep the scope of the work and your progress firmly in focus. Having a syllabus helps you to get out of your comfort zones and step into the more uncomfortable areas of preparation as you move ahead. It is a ready reckoner and helps you in allotting your time to the tasks at hand. If there is no syllabus, then make one. List down all the topics and sub-topics that you can think of in a particular subject and then update it periodically. With this little work, you will get a huge edge on everyonc else who is driving around without a route map.
4. **Develop a project-oriented approach:** The most frequent question that is put up to any student who has achieved success is "how many hours of study did you put in every day?" While this question does have its merits, it is essentially

incomplete. The correct question would be, "how many hours of study did you put in every day and what was your output?" The merit of this question is much more than that of the former. As a student you may sit on your study table for eight hours at a stretch and not finish one topic/ chapter of your syllabus. In such a scenario, you end up with a false feeling of achievement at having spent your time gainfully in pursuit of your goal when, in reality, you have wasted it. Such an approach ultimately leads to failure, which in turn reinforces the belief in you that success is a matter of luck rather than design.

While it is correct to measure your progress in the number of hours spent on the job, it must also be quantified in terms of the amount of work done in those hours. Real output is achieved when effectiveness is backed with efficiency. The fact that you are spending time on achieving your goal means that you are effective. But it does not help unless and until you are efficient also. Efficiency means extracting the maximum output from a given resource. In your case the resource is time. Every minute has to be accounted for and made to count. To quote Rudyard Kipling, "If you can fill the unforgiving minute with sixty seconds worth of distance run, Yours is the earth and everything that is in it, and what's more, You'll be a man my son!". Very correctly he has used the term "unforgiving" for the minute. Time is a very unforgiving resource and is exceedingly finite. It has to be utilised to the fullest extent.

Doing one hour worth of work in eight hours is nothing but wastage. It is better to work for one hour, extract the correct mileage and spend the rest of the time in some other activity. The best way to utilize the time with maximum efficiency is to set daily targets. Once you have set a target for a day, you have to meet it come what may. If it takes more than the allotted hours of work for the day, increase the hours. This will lead to a tremendous sense of self-satisfaction and also help in setting realistic targets which are sufficiently challenging but not unachievable. You should record your progress in a daily diary. Desist from writing anything in this diary except data related to your daily targets and your achievements relative to them. Once you adopt this approach to study, you will find a big change in yourself and will start feeling more like a professional and less like a student. The enhanced control that this method gives you over your time and its utilization will help to usher in a great sense of achievement and confidence. Suddenly the quantum of work will appear less intimidating and more manageable. The only correct approach to study is the project-oriented approach. A time-oriented approach should be immediately abandoned in its favour.

5. **Simulate the real thing:** The word 'Simulation' means as close an approximation of the real conditions as practically possible. While studying, the ultimate purpose of the whole exercise must be kept sharply in focus. Are you

studying for a competitive exam? In that case you have to remember that you will be faced with two main challenges; time pressure and need for accuracy in answering. Whenever you attempt practice tests, you must do so under the same time pressure that you are going to experience in the actual exam and should aim for the same level of accuracy as is required in the real fight. Let us say that the test-paper in the final exam that you are supposed to face will have 150 multiple-choice-type questions and the time allotted for solving them will be 120 minutes. Also let us assume that you will be required to answer the questions by filling up an OMR sheet with an HB pencil. The best way to practice for such a test is to get an OMR sheet from the market or make one for yourself at home and get it photocopied in sufficient numbers. Each time you attempt a practice test, it should be done in a closed room, within the allotted time (120 minutes in this case). Remember, no breaks are allowed. The clock keeps on ticking regardless of what you are doing. Even if you drink a glass of water or go to the toilet, the time is counted within those 120 minutes. This approach will give you the correct picture of the extent of your preparedness for the final exam. Later on you can do the analysis of the paper and look for solutions to the problems you were unable to solve. But the practice test must be attempted as if you were attempting the real test. When you continue this kind of practice, your performance in the practice test will be a very close approximation of your actual performance in the final test. At the same time you will be greatly enhancing your capability of handling time pressure and need for accuracy.

6. **Practice, Practice, Practice:** Merely studies may help you to become a master of the subject, but it may not be sufficient to get you ahead of the competition. That requires an in-depth analysis of the requirements of the exam and an approach that enables you to master them. One condition I have discussed in the preceding point. There are several other types of exams. Some have sections with their own cut-off marks and time slots, others require answers to be written within defined word limits, and still others are attempted online on a computer. Depending upon the kind of exam that you are going to take, you have to re-create similar conditions for your practice and then develop a regular schedule of practice sessions. The more you practice the better equipped you become for the ultimate fight. Any preparation without such an inbuilt practice programme my get you a doctorate in the subject, but will not help you to beat the competition.

Understanding friendship and the value of friends in career-building

It is normal experience that once a person becomes totally involved in the preparation for his or her chosen goal, the time available for socializing and fraternizing reduces drastically. This reduction in time produces friction. Friends and acquaintances demand attention and time. When you are not in a position to devote time to them, they start feeling alienated and even rejected. None of us wants to lose friends. So we start to cut down on the time reserved for preparation and start investing it on our friends. Now, the question is whether this is the right approach?

My answer to this question is "Certainly Not". The best approach to tackle this problem is to sit down with your friends and explain to them that you are preparing for a goal. Make them realize that you are committed and that the goal is very important for you. Tell them your study/practice hours and the best time to call or to meet. Underscore that you are not in a position to be available to them all the time as it will be injurious to your work. If they are truly your friends they will understand. Your goal, your passion should be dear to them also if they are your true friends at all. Their attitude should be nothing but cooperative and encouraging. A 'friend', who insists on wasting your time for his/her happiness, is not a friend, but an enemy. Such 'friends' are actually self-centred and rapacious people who have little or no scruples and are inclined towards using other people's resources for their own benefit. We should remember that such people do not waste their own time. They will complete their own work and when free, will start demanding that you spend your time with them with complete disregard to your priorities. If you refuse to give in to their unreasonable demands, they will use emotional blackmailing to force you to give in to their demands.

Let me illustrate with an example. Let us suppose that you have a friend who runs a shop in a busy market. On a certain day, when the market is open, you happen to be free in the afternoon and decide to watch the movie which has been recently released. You go to the shop of this friend of yours and ask him to accompany you to the movie. He doesn't have to pay. You are footing the bill.

What answer do you expect to such a request? Do you expect that your friend will willingly close his shop and go to the movie with you? Or do you think that his reply will be in the negative? As I see it, this friend of yours will excuse himself by saying, "You know I would love to go to the movie with you. But at the moment I can't leave the shop. The movie has been released only yesterday. Why don't we go on Sunday? You see, the market is closed on Sunday...." As his good friend he will expect you to realize that his time is valuable and closing the shop in the afternoon of a working day will cause him financial loss. And, of course, as a good friend you will understand. If this is true then the converse should also be true. If the time of your friend is valuable at a certain time and date, and he expects you to understand this fact, then your friend should also understand your inability to entertain him at any given time. He should also realize that your time too has a value attached to it and you can't spend it with him as per his requirement.

It is true that such an approach will lead to a good number of such 'friends' making a hasty exit from your life. Far from feeling sorry for the loss of such 'friends,' you should be feeling thankful. Your friends should value your success and appreciate your efforts towards achieving it. Those who are willing to compromise with your success for their own enjoyment are your enemies and you should get rid of them as soon as possible.

Choosing the right friends

I once read a quote. It could also be a Chinese proverb. It was simple and straight and here is what it said. "One who has too many friends has no friends".

Chew on this for a moment. As in all other things of life, quality matters. Suppose I asked you to choose between a basket full of rotten mangoes and a basket containing very few top-class mangoes, which one would you choose? Certainly you won't select the basket full of rotten mangoes? The same goes with relationships. The entire city need not be your friend for you to be a successful person. A few friends with outstanding qualities, consideration for your limitations and devotion for your cause are better, infinitely better, than a slew of friends and acquaintances, who are selfish and are more concerned about furthering their career and happiness than about yours. Of course, once you find the few quality relationships that I am talking about, you must go out of your way to preserve and nurture them. But chances are that such persons and relationships will almost never ask you to go out of your way for their sake.

While looking for new friends it is always better to befriend those who have similar aims and spotless ethics. Such people are few and hard to find, but it is worth looking for them. With such people, there will be no incongruence of priorities and the mutual exchange of time and ideas will be more fruitful and enriching.

Always keep in mind that company matters. It has its effect in subtle ways and this effect is usually not discernable until it becomes overpowering. Rightly has it been said that a person is known by the company he keeps.

Issue of competition between friends with similar aims

'Competition', in my view is the most misunderstood word in the English lexicon. Almost always it is interpreted negatively and selfishly. In fact, it is often taken to be the antonym of 'altruism'. Most students are led to believe that their success equates with the failure of others. Such an attitude, once ingrained in the psyche, leads to the development of a selfish, negative individual who is ill prepared for the final battle. Allow me to illustrate this assertion with the help of an example.

Let us suppose that you are one of a class of fifty students. The competition that the entire class is preparing for requires that a student should secure at least 80% marks in aggregate if at all he/she has to succeed. There are regular practice tests for the class and everybody in the class is repeatedly securing 60% marks except you. You are the only student who is consistently securing 75% marks. You are delighted with your performance and the entire class is jealous of you. It gives you great pleasure to be way ahead of your peers and somewhere, in your heart, you are also happy at their failure, even though you will not admit it openly. You are so happy with your 'achievement' that you go slack. You start taking it easy. You lose sight of the fact that the requirement of competition is a minimum of 80% in aggregate. Content in your performance, you appear in the exam and outdo your self. You score 79% marks in the actual exam and you fail! So does everybody else in the class.

This is the classic mistake that most students make. Such a mistake is a natural outcome of pitching yourself against your peers. It is the obvious result of wrong benchmarking. What is really sad is that it is entirely avoidable.

The key to success in any competition, therefore, is correct benchmarking. The solution is the realization that so far as the competition is concerned, your peers are insignificant. Instead of concentrating on them, the correct approach is to concentrate on yourself. Instead of benchmarking yourself against them it is best to benchmark yourself against the exam. The simple solution is to realize that it is impossible for you to fail if you score 100% marks. That should be the aim. All your energies should be directed towards scoring the maximum possible marks in the final exam, which naturally means 100%. At the same time you should be aware of the trend of the exam and the minimum percentage that is required to clear it. If, in your practice tests, you are falling below the minimum cut-off percentage, you should lose your sleep. It does not matter if all your peers are scoring 40% and you are scoring 75%, you must not feel happy or satisfied. It does not matter whether the score is 40 or 75; in any case it is a failing score. If others are not perturbed with their poor performance, it is their problem. You must constantly strive to score at least ten per cent above the minimum required target. This way, even if everything goes wrong in the final exam and you end up scoring even ten per cent less than you have been scoring in your practice tests, you are still assured of your berth. Contrary to popular belief there is plenty of room at the top. The problem is that there are not many people who are willing to invest all their efforts and energy in climbing the ladder.

Dealing with a broken heart

There are very few of us who fail to get romantically involved during our growing-up years. There are fights, reconciliations, demands and sacrifices. Such relationships are necessarily demanding and emotionally draining. A vast majority of us are unfortunate enough to get trapped in one-sided relationships where the object of our affection has almost as much interest in us as an average person has in the dog sniffing garbage on the road. 'Heartbreak' is the obvious result of such state of affairs, unless we try our very best to win over the person who has chosen to ignore us. Career naturally becomes the last priority in such circumstances. The person who is spurned in love and also ends up as a failure in life has a convenient excuse to explain his or her downfall. I use the word 'excuse' because anyone who is genuinely in love will never fail in life. Need a reason? I will give you one.

Let me ask you a basic question. Why would you fall in love with anyone? How simple, you would say. Obviously that someone would have to be really special. Allow me to rephrase. Suppose you love somebody, and I asked you the reason of your affection for that somebody, what would you say? Unless and until I am too mistaken, the gentleman would answer that the lady he loves is beautiful, intelligent, confident, affectionate, well educated, cultured, career oriented (optional), and understanding. He would, in all probability, add that she makes him feel like a man. The lady, on the other hand, would say that the gentleman she adores is handsome, intelligent, witty, career minded (compulsory), caring, very confident and makes her feel like a lady. In short, both the sexes would look for a set of attributes in their opposite sex. Almost certainly, none of them would say that they like someone because he/she is like a lovelorn, whimpering puppy, pleading with sad and forlorn eyes with a look of mendicancy on his/her face. That is the point. No matter how hard you try, you cannot win over anyone unless and until you develop within your personality certain magnetism and a certain set of attributes which are universally desirable and sought after. Such attributes are developed through sustained efforts towards the achievement of goals in life. To chase a person who is ignoring you is the surest way to lose that person. Chasing will only irritate/intimidate him/her. It is the quick recipe for assured failure in love. The only, I repeat; only way to impress the person you covet, is to impress upon that person that you are a master of your emotions. Go ahead and bare your heart to him or her, and then go back to your career. In fact, when you are spurned in love, you should work doubly hard to achieve your career-goals. It will serve twin purposes. One, it will give you the much needed distraction to drown your immediate sorrow and two, it will send a message to the other person that you are no lovelorn puppy. Always remember, nobody likes a doormat. So it is best not to become one!

Heartbreak can also come due to other factors like family, (Father, Mother, Siblings, and Relatives), friends, colleagues, superiors, subordinates, neighbours etc. Almost everybody who you are in contact with and who holds some value in your life has the capacity to hurt you. The intensity of the pain may be different but nonetheless, the pain will be there. Being hurt by anyone you love or value will necessarily result in anger and feelings of vengefulness. At times you may even feel like causing physical pain to the culprit and at other times you may feel like ending your own life. Such feelings are the result of unfulfilled and unfocused anger. In such a situation you end up feeling hopeless and depressed. To you, as the victim, the situation may appear utterly hopeless and insurmountable, but, in reality, such a situation offers a rare and valuable opportunity.

Anger is one of the most powerful emotions known to man. It is a classic response of the human organism to a situation of extreme stress wherein the body and mind prepare themselves for extreme measures which a person would, ordinarily, refrain from attempting. Anger is the opposite of fear. In the face of a stressful situation, the response of the organism is to fight or to run. In psychological terms it is known as the "fight or flight" response. If the stressor gives rise to fear, the flight response kicks in and the stressed person flees from the situation. If, however, the stressor results in anger then the stressed person faces the situation and fights. This kind of a clean-cut stimulus-response mechanism works best in lower animals. In humans, however, there are shades of grey. That is because humans possess a unique property called intellect. Intellect is perhaps the strongest power known to man, because it has the ability to modify and override the innate responses of an organism produced by nature. Combined with intellect, a situation of extreme stress becomes a situation of unparalleled opportunity. In a situation where anger is shimmering inside you, your body and mind acquire can uncommon strength. It is true that the immediate response is to vent this strength in a rapid and uncontrolled burst of action. However, such a response is destructive. The power of anger is like nuclear power, which, when allowed to explode, is extremely destructive whereas if properly harnessed, it can produce enough energy to light up a million homes. So, if you are angry, you are powerful. All you need to do is to apply your intellect. Remember, your intellect is stronger than your anger. If your anger is like a horse then your intellect is a skilful rider. Using this rider, you can harness the energy of the horse in the direction of realization of your goals. Whoever has hurt you does not want to see you prosper. Your rise in life can and will be the biggest slap on the face of such a person. If you allow your anger and frustration to destroy your career then you will only play into the hands of the unscrupulous enemy who has hurt you. The moment you allow your anger to destroy your intellect, you allow him/her to win. Channelising the energy produced by the stressor towards the fulfilment of your career dreams can help you to achieve them much quicker. I agree that heartbreak is a serious problem, but for the hard nut, it is also a serious opportunity!

Achieving success in the absence of suitable contacts

This is one statement I would not entirely disagree with. Contacts do help. Knowing the right people in the right places can do wonders for your career. But getting to know the right people is also a part of the career building strategy. The problem is that most people forget that it is only a part of the strategy and start thinking that it is the strategy. You must always remember that the world works on the principle of quid pro quo. Translated into simple English, this statement means, "you scratch my back and I will scratch yours". Think for a moment. Why would someone really influential want to help you? Either it is because you can do something for him in return for his favour or that he sees some potential in you or by a rare chance, he just happens to like you. Ultimately it is once again a question of certain attributes and you as an aspiring career person have to develop such attributes before any right person in the right place takes you seriously.

And then, presuming that you do find such a person who is also willing to help you, the maximum he can do is to get you that coveted admission, or that dream break, or that out-of-turn promotion. The point is that he can help you over the starting line. But once you are over it, you are again on your own. The right person in the right place can help you attain success, but he can never help you retain it. Most persons, who attain success through this route, usually experience a crash which is more humiliating, nightmarish and terrifying than a few small falls on the road to self achieved success. And what's more, here we are talking about an ideal situation. We are presuming that the person who is helping you will be capable and resourceful enough to remove all hurdles from your path in single sweep of his hand. In practice it is not so. Actually what you will find is that the well-connected gentleman batting for you can only help you marginally. He may be able to help you in the interview stage, but you still have to clear the written exam. He may introduce you to the director of the film, but it is you who will have to qualify in the screen test.

I have often come across students who complain that they were rejected in an interview because someone else was selected on the strength of a solid political push in his/her favour. This is the best way to deceive one's own self. The fact of the matter is that such approaches may affect the chances of the candidate at the margins but they have absolutely no effect on the outstanding candidate. An outstanding candidate will get his or her chance, regardless of all the pushes and pulls in favour of his peers. What is even more important is that a candidate who is selected on his own merit is always the one viewed more favourably by his/her peers and superiors. He enjoys a prestige that reinforces his self belief and drives him towards still greater achievement. Once a man stands on his own feet he can jog, run and jump. However a person who is standing with the help of crutches can at best hobble along at a snail's pace. Which one of the two you wish to be, is a matter of personal choice.

Developing the 'something' called 'personality'

The 'something' that I am talking about is a superset

called 'personality'. It is a very wide term encompassing attributes such as education, language, diction, sense of dress, manners, mannerisms, versatility, efficiency, ethics and physical appearance (which includes physique and grooming). Any person aiming to be successful in life must work on all these aspects of his personality in order to make himself stand out among the crowd. Personality, fortunately or unfortunately, is a product of many years of upbringing and grooming. Once it is concretized, very little can be done to alter its basics. However the good news is that given a few basics, a lot can be done to improve it. But before any improvement can be brought about in any personality, we must try and understand what is meant by the attributes listed above.

(a) Education: "Education is what remains behind when all that we have learnt has been forgotten". I really don't know who said this, but it certainly drives home the point. Most of us mistake education for literacy. This is incorrect. Literacy merely means the ability to read and write. Somebody may have very high literacy levels but almost non-existent education. I say this because education in the real sense goes much beyond the ability to read and write. To be educated does not translate into being well-read. It actually translates into being well-developed. Real education widens your horizons. It makes you a better person. It increases your mental capabilities and makes you able to handle new information and challenging situations using mental flexibility and adaptability. True education makes the mind an extremely adaptable faculty. At the same time education imparts a high sense of morality. It develops the mind in the right direction. Literacy or information may be ethical or unethical, but it is education which enables the mind to discern the difference between the two. An educated person is well informed, confident, and ethical.

(b) **Ethics:** This is perhaps the most abstract attribute to understand. To a layman this word could mean 'That what is good'. But again, the word 'good' has no real definition. It is situational. What is good in one situation would be bad in the other. An example can illustrate this point better. Take the case of telling a lie. Perhaps there is universal agreement on the point that lying is certainly not good. But is this universal agreement correct or practical or merely theoretical in nature? Allow me to give you a choice. Suppose you are party to a secret that is vital to the interests of your nation and people. If divulged to an enemy state it has the potential to destroy the fabric of your nation. Now suppose you are captured by an enemy country and interrogated so that they can gain the information from you. What would you do in such a circumstance? Would you do what is accepted as universally good, i.e. speak the truth and subject your nation to danger? Or would you lie in order to protect your country? I feel that the answer to this question would be unanimous. Of course in such a situation, speaking the truth would be the epitome of evil. So, suddenly what is good becomes evil because of the situation. Thus, 'ethics' does not translate into 'good.' So if ethics does not translate into good then what does it mean? I feel that it is the ability to identify what is correct. Again the word 'correct' needs to be defined. I will define it as an option that serves the larger interest. In my book, being ethical means being unselfish. It means being able to ignore narrow personal interests when bigger issues of public well-being are at stake. Such personal interest could range from financial to spiritual. If you possess such strength of character, you will be perceived as an ethical person and will be sought after by organizations. You will be trustworthy and dependable. These two attributes "trustworthiness and dependability" are direct outcomes of a person with a solid foundation of ethics as I have discussed above. Once you possess these, your personality acquires a rare depth which automatically opens doors of opportunities for you.

(c) **Courage:** Just as a building is useless without a solid foundation, a personality is hollow without courage. At the very outset I must caution you that the term 'courage' must not be confused with aggression, violence or foolhardiness. While aggression, violence and foolhardiness are almost always negative traits; courage is never a negative quality. It is a defining characteristic of the soul. You need not have physique like Arnold Schwarzenegger in order to be courageous. In fact, you needn't even have a complete and normal body and brain for the same. What you really need is strength of character. A courageous person is distinguished as having conviction and faith. At the same time such a person should be willing to sacrifice and suffer personal hardships in order to act upon his conviction and save his faith. Again, you need not be Bill Gates or L N Mittal in order to be perceived as courageous. Just as muscle has nothing to do with courage, money also has little connection with it. In my book, a rickshaw puller is a courageous man. It is true that he survives at the bottom of the ladder. But compare him to a beggar and you will understand what I mean. The rickshaw puller could have easily resorted to begging for his livelihood. That would have been much easier (and perhaps much more profitable!) But yet he chooses to do harsh physical labour and earn his livelihood rather than beg for it. I think that we will all unanimously agree that what prevents him from leading a sub-human (even sub-animal) existence of a beggar is his conviction that begging is not what a human being should do in order to keep body and soul together. In order to act upon his conviction he chooses the path of physical labour rather than the much easier but humiliating option of begging. That is why such a person is courageous in my book. Thus, in the ultimate analysis, courage is about the choices we make. Whenever a person makes a choice that is difficult compared to the other choices at hand-which are not ethical, he is exhibiting courage. The student, who refuses to cheat when all others are doing so, is a courageous person. So is an officer who refuses to be corrupt when pressurised/enticed to do so. To have faith in one's own abilities and to go on when there is no end in sight is also a mark of courage. The situations may vary, so may the impact and the outcome, but one thing is common to all courageous men. That attribute is the willingness to suffer adversity for the sake of one's conviction and faith even when other easier options are available.

(d) Grooming: You must have heard the saying "never judge a book by its cover". Very true. I most certainly agree with this saying. But equally true is the fact that the cover matters! By the term 'cover' I mean 'packaging'. It is no doubt essential to have good attributes. But it is equally essential to package them well. It is innate human tendency to be attracted to things which are neat, and well presented. This applies as universally to human beings as it does to goods and services. In order to be attractive to others, at least prima facie, it is important to be well packaged. The human equivalent of a well packaged good is a well groomed exterior. Good grooming reflects in every thing that is visible on the outside; be it your hair, nails, clothes, teeth, shoes, watch, handkerchief, pen, whiskers or the works. All these and everything else that can be noticed by someone on your exterior should be tasteful and should reflect class. Please remember that I am not asking you to become straight jacketed. I mean you would look funny in a discotheque wearing a lounge suit. But, then, you would look equally funny in a professional interview, or a business meeting wearing a jeans and a T-shirt. Well groomed people are like magnets that attract admiring glances where ever they go. Good grooming hides physical attributes that may be unattractive and highlights those that are attractive. It is absolutely essential in order to make a success out of the first impression. First impression may not be the last impression but it certainly is the lasting impression. A good first impression is that which gives you that little bit of leverage and an edge over others who fail in this sphere. In a world where every mark counts, this little edge may define the difference between success and failure, selection and rejection, acceptance and derision. So if you desire to develop a powerful personality, learn to be well groomed. Learn good manners. Develop taste. Be observant. Try to analyse the plus points in the grooming of people whom you find attractive. Ask for help in this sphere. Go to a finishing school if required. Discuss the issue with parents, teachers and seniors. Start taking pride in your appearance. Mind it, I am not asking you to become obsessed. Nor am I exhorting you to become straight jacketed. What I am suggesting is that you devote some time and energy towards making your own self look good. Doing this will make you feel good which in turn will instil confidence in you and bring a smile to your face and a spring in your step. Suddenly you will find people around you reacting more favourably to you. Go ahead. Try it. It works!

(e) **Hobbies Interests:** This is one part of a personality which is as mysterious as it is important. Loosely translated, in colloquial terms, it can also be called 'extra curricular activity'. These are things or activities we do apart from our usual routine work. Almost any activity in this world could be a hobby or an interest. But, before we proceed any further, it is important to understand the difference between a 'hobby' and an 'interest'. An interest is an activity which we pursue for the sake of recreation and self satisfaction. However, we do not actively seek out time for this purpose. Nor do we take any academic interest in the same. Time and occasion permitting, we may participate in or pursue our activity of interest, otherwise not. Hobby, on the other hand is a different ball game altogether. It is all consuming. It is a passion. It is something for which we actively set aside time and seek opportunity. A hobby is also necessarily academic in nature. In fact, usually, an individual pursuing a hobby actively ends up knowing more about his or her hobby than his/her regular occupation. You could say that a hobby is an interest with a big dose of passion thrown in. But the real question here is that how and in what way does an interest or a hobby contribute to a personality? If I were to answer this question, I would say that each such activity (in particular, hobby) adds an additional facet to a personality. A personality can be viewed as a diamond. It is a well known fact that a well cut diamond with a high number of facets is more brilliant than a diamond that is of equal quality but is not so well cut or has lesser number of facets. Consequently the former commands much more value than the latter in the open market. Let us not forget that the core (quality of material) in both the cases remains the same. Now try and apply this analogy to a personality. The personality of a person with a number of facets attains a brilliance that sets him apart from people of equal calibre. Such a personality is called 'multifaceted' and is instantly recognized as one of a superior quality. Moreover, having hobbies helps an individual to broaden his horizons and to relax and enjoy his leisure. It also drives one towards extraction of leisure from busy schedules and goes a long way towards preventing a deadly disorder called 'workaholism'. It also gives one something to look forward to when one retires from active working life. Sometimes a hobby can also develop to such an extent that it becomes a career in itself. There are examples of a doctor becoming a singer (Dr. Palash Sen), a chartered accountant becoming a famous film director (Shekhar Kapoor) and a manager becoming the biggest screen idol ever in India (Amitabh Bachchan). These are the three examples which come readily to my mind. There must be innumerable other such examples in India and abroad. You may even know a few such people. So, in that sense having a hobby also provides you with a career option to be explored and developed at your own leisure. Besides, they always say that the happiest man is the one whose hobby becomes his occupation!

(f) **Manners:** This is another part of a personality that is abstract, yet tangible. It has the power to make or mar the effects of all the previously discussed ingredients of a personality. It is the finishing touch, the proverbial icing on the cake. Again, loosely translated, 'manners' may be understood as 'good behaviour'. But, pointedly, it is much more than mere good behaviour. It is the outward projection of your entire personality. Your words, your body language, sense of humour, process of interaction with others, value systems; all combine and show up in your mannerisms.

These come into play at the time of social and official interactions and help to make you acceptable or unacceptable to your peers, juniors and superiors alike. We have all grown up with our elders telling us to cultivate good manners, but not many of us are aware of what constitutes 'good manners'. To me at least, good manners mean 'behaviour that is in consort with the situation at hand'. Allow me to illustrate. Suppose you meet an enemy in a social setting—say a marriage party. You will be justified in feeling aggressive towards him. But allowing that aggression to surface in such a setting would constitute bad manners. It is all right if you feel that you should shoot your enemy (though of course, forgiveness is more desirable). But it is not all right to give vent to your feelings in such a situation. You should rather control your feelings so that the party is not disturbed and your host is not inconvenienced. I would also stress that good manners mean avoiding extreme behaviour most of the time. Good manners also mean developing a finesse and sense of class along with a sense of propriety as I have discussed above. It means being able to be polite and firm at the same time. Last but not the least, good manners mean gaining knowledge of local customs and practices. A person with good manners is perceived as being well bred and is accepted by his friends and admired by his foes.

The effect of company

"Well the discussion on personality was interesting, but how" you may ask, "how am I expected to acquire so many attributes?" I accept this as a valid question. Different people would have different answers to this question. Some would recommend books, others teachers and guides. But my answer to this question is straightforward. "It all depends upon the company you keep." In the Mahabharata, the greatest Indian epic, there is a story where a yaksha (ghost) poses a number of questions to Yudhishthir, the eldest and wisest of the five Pandavas. In this story Yudhishthir had to answer all the questions of the yaksha correctly, failing which the yaksha would kill him. Among the other questions there was one seminal question. The Yaksha asked Yudhishthir the definition of happiness. To this question the wise pandava replies, "Satsang". This is a Hindi word which can be precisely translated into 'Good Company' (Sat=good, Sang=company). Obviously from times immemorial, the value of good company has never been lost to wise men. We all must have come across the English saying, "a man is known by the company he keeps (equally true for women also!)" So, a strong and pleasant personality is acquired not so much by the road you choose to travel on but by who your companions are on that road. The human mind is the most pliable object on earth. It is also the most sensitive receiver and the strongest recorder of information. We gather information not just through our eyes and ears, but through all our five senses. At the same time much more information is gathered and stored passively than is done actively. If you tend to disagree with this assertion, pause for a moment and try to recall when and how you memorised the roads of your city. If I am right, you will only recall that somehow, over the years, you just happened to memorise the same without really making an effort to do so. If an inanimate and boring object as a road can imprint itself irreversibly on your mind, imagine the effect of human company! We inadvertently and irreversibly absorb the attributes of those whose company we keep, over a period of time. In fact, a research shows that husbands and wives start to resemble each in the later stages of life and another research shows that people even begin to resemble their pet dogs!

If company has such extreme and perceptible effects on our personality, then it is a matter of only a minor inconvenience if you have to go and seek out good people and strive to remain in their company. Mind you, I am not asking you to become a recluse or antisocial. Socializing is one thing and companionship quite the other. A friend or companion is a person with whom you spend more time than you would ordinarily spend with someone else. You share your thoughts, your feelings, your hobbies, your fortunes and your misfortunes with a companion. I strongly advise you to seek out people with strong personalities. The word 'strong' must not be interpreted as 'extreme'. Having read the portion on personality, you are now aware of the attributes that you have to look for while choosing a friend or companion. Chances are that you won't have to dissect a person to find such attributes. Rather an individual in possession of sterling qualities will automatically impress you to such an extent that you start seeking his company. While stressing on the importance of company I am not trying to belittle the importance of other influences and inputs that help in shaping a superior personality. They should be utilized to the fullest extent possible. It's only that, in my opinion, the effects of good or bad company override the effects of all other inputs.

The habit of reading

"To be or not to be, that is the question". This was the old line. Perhaps in today's world the new line should say "to read or not to read." It seems ironical but in the age of information technology, the biggest casualty has been information itself. By 'information' I mean quality information. I remember, when we were kids, reading was a big rage. From comic books to children's novels, one was practically an outcast if one was not 'in' with one's reading. There was no internet and mobile phone and television used to air just one channel. So the chief source of information in those years was books, magazines and newspapers. These also provided the bulk of the entertainment (the other source of the same being sports). Libraries flourished and possession of quality books used to be a status symbol. Sadly, all this has undergone a radical change which seems more negative than positive. The onslaught by various media has slowly but steadily squeezed out the printed word from its position as the preferred medium of information. Today I find that most of the students and even young adults are poorly read. There is extreme over-reliance on the audio-visual media and even their use is mostly wasteful in nature. While the reading habit has declined, its importance in the success of an individual most certainly hasn't. Any person wishing to be successful in life ***has*** to read. The minimum that you are expected to read every day is one quality newspaper. Apart from that every well bred person must aspire to develop his own personal library. This library should contain high quality books on the field of his study or occupation as well as those on subjects relating to his hobbies and interests. Dictionaries on terms relating to economics and science are also desirable. I expect a well read person to have some grasp of history (both national and international), philosophy and literature. Besides it is important to follow some magazines of national stature for a good understanding of current affairs of national and international importance. OK! I know what you are going to say. "I am a sportsperson, so why should I read all the stuff that you have mentioned. Or for that matter, why should I read at all?" The answer is that the importance of being well read is universal in nature. While I don't deny the fact that it may be more important for those who are in office jobs and careers, I also don't accept the assertion that it is not required for those who are in other fields such as sports and performing arts. The purpose of reading is not so much to gain information as it is to develop a mature, receptive and analytical mind. Reading good books exposes you to new ideas. It develops your vocabulary and power to assimilate and express. Reading does to the mind what a gymnasium does to the body. It tones and strengthens the brain and keeps it young. I am sure that such a brain is an asset in any field, be it office, sports or performing arts. If you still disagree take a look around you. Most of the people you will find at the top in any field will be well read and well informed individuals. So in case you are not reading, you are doing a positive disservice to yourself and reducing your chances of developing a strong personality, and, as a consequence, your chances of success. Now the next question is how and when to read? As regards 'how', I would say that the best method of reading is scanning followed by concentrated reading. When you open a new book, the first thing that you should do is to flip through the pages/chapters right to the end. This activity is called 'scanning'. Scanning familiarizes you with the book and makes it less intimidating. Once you have done the scanning the reading can follow. While scanning may not be so important when reading light text (like a novel), it is vital while reading heavy text containing hard information and loads of data.

Reading must always be done with a calm mind and with an intention to enjoy rather than to cram. The focus must always be to grasp the central idea of the author. Most of us commit the mistake of focusing on the words. It's a bit like going on an African Safari and all the time staring at the seat of the vehicle when you should be enjoying the real sights outside the window. Words, you must remember, are nothing more than this vehicle. They merely serve to put down an idea on paper. Trying to cram the words or language of the author translates into time and effort gone waste. There are several good books available which spell out the techniques of effective reading. Do consult such books. Take help from persons who seem to flip through text and yet comprehend and retain the ideas. Effective and efficient reading is something to be practiced and learnt just like playing a musical instrument. The more you practice, the better you will become.

Having discussed 'how', we must not turn to 'when'. The good thing is that so far as the habit of reading is concerned, there is nothing called 'when'! It's a matter of personal choice. No time or place is too outlandish for reading. Still, for the sake of suggestion, I will stress that early morning is the best time to read. Reading is also best avoided when you are expected to concentrate on other matters of immediate urgency. For instance, a soldier on the front facing a barrage of bullets from the enemy would be acting with stupidity if he decides to read a motivational book at that very moment. In doing so, chances are that he would not remain alive to act on whatever motivation he derived from that book! Similarly, avoid reading magazines secretly during meetings or lectures. Such reading is not reading but a time wasting tactic and does nothing in terms of broadening your thoughts or furthering your career.

Barring this, reading can be done in any spare time that you have when you are not required to concentrate on any thing else. It could be during travel (provided you yourself are not driving), during the wait for your turn at the doctor's chamber, or even in the toilet! The basic argument is that any reading is better than no reading. So go ahead. Start reading today and embark on your road to success.

The value of adversity

Being human, all of us dread adversity. The mere thought that 'something going wrong' is unsettling and even terrifying. And I, for one, being human like the rest of us, couldn't agree more. Adversity is stressful and often demeaning and humiliating. So, I do not blame you for going out of your way to avoid meeting this ghost head-on. But pause for a moment and think. Is 'adversity' really such a negative attribute in our lives? Is it really something to be avoided like the plague? Or is there a positive side to it also?

Let us pause to think. We tend to use words like 'adversity', 'calamity' and 'disaster' as synonyms. But are they really synonyms? I think not. To put it slightly mathematically, I could say that adversity is a superset of which calamity and disaster are subsets. In plain English, this means that all calamities and disasters are adversities but not all adversities are calamities or disasters. And here lies the catch. While I do not advocate the subsets, I will certainly speak in favour of the superset. But before I move ahead let us try and understand what the word 'adversity' means.

Adversity is a condition when things, events, or situations force us to step out of our comfort zones. 'Comfort Zone' is a term which denotes all conditions which, when existing, prevent us from feeling stressed or challenged. For instance, if you are used to sleeping on a certain kind of bed with a certain kind of mattress and pillow, you would not, ordinarily want to sleep on some other bed. So, for the purpose of sleep and the kind of bed you are used to become your comfort zone. The moment you are forced to change any parameter of the bed you are stepping out of your comfort zone and creating an adverse situation for your sleep. In effect, the mere change of bed is a minor adversity! Similarly, anything that makes you feel less than absolutely comfortable can safely be put under the heading of 'adversity'. Of course the impact of the adversity on your comfort level, and, therefore, the cognisance that you take of the same may vary. But the definition remains true no matter how small the impact. So, for the sake of argument, I can safely say that the most comfortable condition, a condition with zero adversity, is the one where you are lying on your favourite bed in your favourite room with the air conditioner running silently, doing whatever you enjoy the most (from reading to watching TV to surfing the net to sleeping). Or, to rephrase, I could say that the condition of least adversity is one where you are doing your favourite activity in your preferred surroundings. But suppose I said that you had no choice but to perform your favourite activity in your preferred surroundings ad-infinitum. That is, once you started doing it you would have no choice but to keep on doing it for the rest of your life. Would it still appear as rosy and comfortable as it appears now? I guess not. You would get terribly bored. Eventually you would want a change. And, in order to get the change, you would have to step out of your comfort-zone. And, it is from this point that the central argument originates. The argument is, "Adversity is not negative. In fact it is so valuable that at times it has to be actively sought out"

Now, let us try and understand the argument. I mean, how in the blazes could adversity be positive and valuable? How could stress be important? After all, isn't the whole purpose of life the pursuit of comfort and happiness?

Allow me to answer. Think for a moment of the most helpless and innocent thing in this world. To my mind it has to be a newborn baby. If there is someone or something, which deserves to be absolutely comfortable and happy, it is a newborn. But what do we do hours after the baby is out of the womb? We pierce a needle into its delicate skin and give it a shot of a vaccine! Now, just look at it from the point of view of the baby. In the space of a few minutes it gets thrown out violently from the secure place that was its home for good nine months. It is forced to breathe on its own. And as if that was not enough it is pierced with a needle when it is most stressed!! I would say that from the point of view of the baby the situation is not of adversity, it is calamity! Left on its own, the baby would never want to step out of the womb where it was getting nourishment without having to open its mouth, and where the living conditions were so good that even gravity was not a problem! But would that position of comfort be good for the baby? Obviously it would not. The baby has to come out in this world, face discomfort, face the pain of vaccination, brave the elements and in general a big load of adversity if at all it has to survive and become a successful adult.

Think about how you grew up. Being made to attend classes in the school was adversity. Having to appear in exams was a bigger adversity. Falling from the bicycle and breaking a wrist-bone was adversity. Crashing dad's car while learning to drive on the sly was a bigger adversity. Telling dad about the accident was calamity! But you endured all that and more. And now, on hindsight, I am sure that you feel that you are what you are because you faced all the adversity and hardship head-on instead of running away from it.

The fact of the matter, thus, is that adversity is not

only desirable; it is an essential ingredient of success. I could quote any number of examples to illustrate this point. But the most important example is evolution itself. Charles Darwin, the father of modern theory of evolution has proved it beyond any doubt that it is the adversity created by environmental conditions that forces species to change and adapt. In the process, the old species are replaced by new more robust species which are more in tune with their surroundings and, consequently, more successful.

The Darwinian principle of adaptability has to be kept in focus when facing adverse circumstances. If the situations can be changed to one's own advantage, they should be changed, otherwise it is best to change one's own self in accordance with the demands of the situation. In any case, adversity must be viewed as a process of development and learning. Our body does it all the time. Every day we are exposed to new pathogens. Some cause disease and the others are vanquished by the immune system before they can turn virulent. However each such exposure strengthens the immune system of the body to the extent that subsequent exposure to the same pathogen fails to cause a disease. Facing disease is a big adversity. But it is the only way to learn how to combat it successfully. A baby placed in a sterile environment and allowed to grow to adulthood would die from a slew of diseases the moment it was allowed to step out of such an environment.

The key is to understand that there is no situation or environment, which may be static. Change is the only constant in this universe. Any change, which is adverse in nature, is not so much of a problem as it is an opportunity. Keeping a positive attitude towards such changes in life and learning ways and means to cope with them strengthens us and contributes vastly towards success in life. So, don't shun adversity. Face it. In fact, I will go to the extent of saying that, once in a while, go ahead and seek it actively. Do it for the simple reason that adversity is valuable!

The importance of strategic retreat

We are all products of the thought that surrender is for weaklings. The only way for a man to function is to stand up and fight. I totally agree with this presumption. Fight we must. But before we enter into a fight we must stop and think!

I am sure that you must be aware of the name of Lord Krishna. He was one of the greatest warriors of his time and was never vanquished in battle. But the lesser-known fact is that he ran away from more battles than what he actually fought! For this reason he is also known as '*Ranchhod Das*'. Translated into English this means 'one who runs away from battles'. So how in the world could someone who had a reputation for running away from battles be hailed as a great warrior? The answer is simple. Krishna had the intelligence and the foresight to identify which battles were worth fighting.

I once read a saying. It goes like this. "I learnt a long time ago never to fight with a pig. Your clothes get dirty and the pig likes it!" And therein lie the crux. To fight is important. But it is even more important to distinguish between real battles and useless feuds. It is also equally important to evaluate one's own resources and win ability before entering into a fight. If the situation is hopeless and you know that it is a fight that you cannot hope to win, it is better to escape rather than to perish. It is not only useless, but even foolish, to die in the pursuit of the impossible. The better option is to get out of such a situation, marshal your resources, gain time and strength, ponder over whether it would be fruitful to go back and fight again, and then, if you still feel that it is worth the effort and the risk, give it your best shot backed by all your strength, resources and planning. Critics might call such action 'cowardice' but I think that it is the epitome of bravery. Nothing is braver than the willingness to accept temporary defeat if it is a stepping stone on the road to ultimate victory. Sacrifice should be commensurate with the expected outcome. If you are sure that your death will ensure survival of your people and your nation, then surrender is not an option. But, on the contrary, if you know that self-sacrifice will be an unnecessary act of bravado with no tangible benefit to the cause at hand, then surrender is the only option. In addition to being a soldier, be a tactician, and, pretty soon, you will find yourself in the seat of the General!

Punctuality–a way of life

If you were to ask me what separates a successful man from an unsuccessful person or a developed nation from a 'developing economy', my answer would be 'punctuality'. In this context, it is best to quote Rudyard Kipling, the Noble Prize winning author. ***"If you can fill the unforgiving minute with sixty seconds worth of distance run, Yours is the earth and every thing that is in it, And what's more, You will be a man my son!"*** The value of this singular attribute has never been lost to those who wish to be or are successful in life. The underlying concept of punctuality is not the saving of a few minutes. Rather the bedrock of the attribute is 'respect'. A person who is punctual is necessarily respectful. A punctual person realizes the value of time. He/she is acutely aware that the only true resource in this universe is time. Such a person is never late for a meeting, a class or a gathering because of the realization that such a delay will result in the wastage of the time of others. It's the inherent respect for others and their resources that makes a person punctual. Since 'respect' is a cultural phenomenon, to me punctuality is also a product of the culture of a country. A good example to quote in this connection is that of the Japanese. Japan is one nation where respect (for self and for others) is a major cultural trait. Consequently the Japanese are perhaps the most punctual people on this planet. The fallout of their respect for time is an exemplary level of efficiency. Their system runs like clockwork. Trains arrive and depart dot on time. Nobody has to wait for anybody to arrive in a meeting. The result of this culture of respect is that one of the most densely populated nations in this world saves millions of man-hours per day which would otherwise have been lost due to lack of punctuality. It is this culture of punctuality that has enabled the Japanese to develop a method of management that is known as 'Just-In-Time'. This method of management ***eliminates*** inventories. Elimination of inventories from industry means a saving of billions of dollars per year for business. It is just one example of how punctuality can redefine the way in which economies of nations function.

What is true at a national level is also true at a personal level. Along with respect, another important dimension of punctuality is 'discipline'. Punctuality cannot be achieved in the absence of discipline. A culture of punctuality generates a culture of discipline. One who wishes to be punctual ***has*** to be self-disciplined. Self-discipline, once inculcated has a spill over effect. It is, therefore, hardly surprising that in a punctual nation, systems start functioning smoothly. The little roadblocks to success that emerge due to little and almost invisible transgressions of rules and regulations get ironed out automatically. Crowds on counters automatically get transformed into queues. Order replaces chaos and results start emerging from deliberations. "Sixty seconds worth of distance run" starts getting extracted from every minute that is spent.

In the chapter where I have discussed the correct way to study, I have introduced the concept of time being a currency. The net result of punctuality is a saving and a productive use of this currency. Even the most cynical of us realize that the fastest way to get rich is to simultaneously get the best productivity from our money and to save as much as possible in the process. The only way to apply this principle to the currency called 'time' is to be punctual. Once a person adopts and inculcates the culture of punctuality in his/her way of life, the savings are immediately obvious. The same 24 hours in the day appear enough for everything, be it work, family and leisure. Personal efficiency shoots up. Stress levels drop. The Happiness quotient skyrockets and respect within the society and peers takes a quantum jump. Professionally, a punctual person is perceived as an "I-

Mean-Business" Personality. Superiors tend to rely on such a person and subordinates look up to him/her with admiration and awe. What are unachievable deadlines for others become normal and achievable targets for such a person. Achieving targets is ultimately what success is all about! So you see punctuality is not something that you pay for. Rather it pays to be punctual. So what's stopping you? Just go ahead and adopt this way of life and reap the benefits for all times to come!

An invaluable resource called "Anger"

So you are angry? You have solid reasons to feel infuriated with everybody and everything. Dad does not understand you. Mom has too many expectations. Siblings are selfish. Friends are judgemental. Boss has his priorities all wrong. The world at large is mean. In short, nothing is right! You feel like setting everything on fire or blowing up the whole world or running away to some place where people would be more rational. Yes you *are* angry! And let me share a secret with you. In case you feel this way, you are not alone. Most of us feel this way at least at some time or the other. So in that sense, welcome to the club! 'Anger' we are often told, is one letter short of 'Danger'. This very powerful human emotion is always presented as a negative trait, as something to be wary of and shunned. But look at it again. Is it really so negative? I mean anger is one of the countless emotions that we feel. If we cannot remove emotions like love, sympathy, happiness etc. from our psyches then how can we even think of getting rid of anger? So, there is no need to get rid of anger. In fact it is to be welcomed. That is because 'anger' is not a liability. It is an asset. It is a resource which is downright invaluable. Want to know why? Let me tell you.

Anger is one of the most innate emotions known to man. It is an emotion we have in common with almost all animals. To that extent it can be termed as an 'instinct' rather than an emotion. 'Anger' is a condition when the animal within us perceives a threat. Such a perception instinctively triggers a chain of physiological and psychological responses within our system. The adrenal glands start pumping out adrenalin and noradrenalin. These hormones are also known as the 'stress hormones'. The effect of the two is to prepare the body and mind for battle. The heart starts pumping faster in order to ensure supply of blood and oxygen to all the muscles of the body. The muscles become taut and ready for explosive action. The mind loses sense of fear. Focus and concentration are increased and the ability of the entire system to perform under stress is increased manifold. Thus, anger is an instinct that prepares the mind and body for the best possible performance under the circumstances. This response occurs in all animals. However, what happens after this cascade of events is what differentiates a human being from an animal.

In a typical animal, say a tiger, the outcome of all this priming is a burst of explosive and destructive activity. An angry tiger will tear its opponent to shreds. Once that happens, the energy built up due to anger is released and the system of the animal returns to normal. The same explosive action takes place in case of humans who are unable to control their anger. An angry man with a gun in his hand, unable to control his anger, will shoot to kill. It is the same act as that of a tiger tearing its adversary to shreds. So, in a nutshell, anger generates unmatched energy in your system. Energy, as we all know is the most valuable resource in this universe. That logically means that an emotion or instinct that generates energy must also be equally valuable. And therein lie the importance of anger.

The energy generated by anger is akin to nuclear energy. If allowed to be released in one uncontrolled explosion, nuclear energy causes untold destruction. However, if channelized, controlled and released gradually, the same energy generates electric power that can light up millions of homes, power industries and lead to unparalleled development. Nuclear energy, by itself, is neither good nor bad. It's the control and use of it that makes it so. Same is the case with anger. The raw energy of anger is a resource that needs to be channelised and used to one's advantage. Utilised in this manner, it can transform an individual and the world around him. I would like to illustrate this point with the help of two examples:

The angry Prime Minister, Kautilya and the Mauryan Empire

Kautilya (also known as Chanakya/Vishnugupta) was born in Patliputra (now Patna in Bihar/India) in BC 350. History records that he was a brilliant but ugly man. At that time the most powerful empire in India was that of the Nanda Kings with Patliputra as their capital. The Nanda monarchy, after ages of rule, had become self-centred and arrogant. One day the then monarch Dhana Nanda, who was much hated and despised by his subjects because of his wickedness, called his prime-minister and insulted him in public. The minister was incensed. However, he controlled his anger and left the court. More than any thing else, the angry prime minister of Dhana Nanda realised that the time had come when a monarchy and dynasty which was so insensitive to its subjects had to be replaced with a new system. One day, while taking a walk in a field, the Prime Minister saw a young Brahmin. The Brahmin was frightfully ugly. He had a sharp metal rod in his hands with which he was exposing the roots of a clump of elephant grass and pouring a whitish liquid into the roots from a pot that he was carrying. Curious about the strange looking Brahmin and his equally strange actions the prime minister walked up to the Brahmin and addressed him.

"O wise Brahmin, my greetings, I am the Prime Minister of this Kingdom"

"Greetings, Prime Minister", replied the Brahmin and went on with his work.

"May I be curious enough to know your name, what you are trying to do and the reason behind your actions?"

"O Prime Minister, I am Kautilya" replied the Brahmin. "I was walking barefoot in this field when a sharp stem from this clump of grass pierced my foot and injured me. I had the option of cutting this clump of grass. But as you know, this is elephant grass and till the roots are alive, no amount of cutting will stop it from regrowing"

"Yes, so...?"

"Since this grass had hurt my foot, I had to ensure its complete destruction. So I am digging up the ground around its roots and pouring sour buttermilk it its roots. The sour buttermilk will kill the roots and ensure that this grass is completely destroyed"

The Prime Minister looked at the young Brahmin in disbelief. Here was a person who was going to such great length to destroy a clump of grass that had hurt his foot!! He had the answer to his problem.

Next day, the Prime Minister took Kautilya to the Nanda Monarch. He introduced him to the monarch as a wise man of great ability and learning. However, as expected, the king, instead of offering a seat and respect to Kautilya, insulted him left and right because he was ugly and ordered him to leave the court. That was exactly what the Prime Minister had expected and wanted the king to do. An insulted and angry Kautilya left the court. Now the mission of his life was to find a man who could overthrow the Nanda Empire. The man he located was called Chandragupta Maurya. The rest, as they say, is history. Under the guidance of Kautilya, Chandragupta Maurya overthrew the Nanda Empire, and founded the Mauryan Dynasty that is, to date, regarded as one of the most successful dynasties of the world. It gave India rulers (apart from Chandragupta Maurya himself) of the stature of Samudragupta (also known as the Napoleon of India) and Ashoka the Great. Kautilya himself went on to be regarded as the greatest political strategist that India had ever seen. His works "Arthashastra"and "Nitishastra" are widely regarded as a must read for anyone wishing to be successful in politics or administration.

As for the angry Prime Minister of the Nanda King, I do not know what became of him. However one thing is clear as crystal. Had that Prime Minster allowed his anger to explode in front of the Nanda Monarch when he was being publicly humiliated and insulted, he would surely have been put in the gallows or beheaded. The ability of the Prime Minister to tolerate the hurt, control his temper in the face of immediate provocation, and then direct the energy generated by the anger towards finding a solution to the problem ultimately led to one of the most monumental and fruitful changes in Indian History.

The angry Barrister and Independence of India from the British

It was the year 1893 when a young man, 24 years of age, boarded a train in South Africa. The name of the man was Mohandas Karamchand Gandhi. He was a barrister from India, educated in England. Dressed like an Englishman, he boarded the first-class compartment of the train and settled down to read a newspaper. At a station called Pietermaritzburg, Gandhi was asked to move to the third class compartment of the train by the conductor and some fellow white passengers. When he protested and said that he was entitled to travel in first class as he was in possession of a valid ticket for the same, he was manhandled and thrown off the train. I guess that all of us would agree that getting thrown off a train, when in possession of a valid ticket, must not have been a pleasant experience at all. Personally at least, I can say that I would have been infuriated had it happened to me. So I will presume that it must have angered young Mohandas Karamchand Gandhi as well. But, Gandhi was no ordinary man. He chose to hold back his anger and complete his journey by other available means. In the process, he suffered even more hardships including being barred from many hotels because he was black in colour! The more Mohandas saw and experienced apartheid and racial discrimination, the angrier he became with the system. Gandhi was in Durban on a contract and was due to return upon the expiry of the contract. But he didn't return. Rather he stayed on in South Africa and tranformed the Indian diaspora in South Africa into a strong political force. Having done seminal work against racial discrimination in South Africa, Gandhi directed the force of his anger towards the issue of independence of India from British rule, (albeit in a non-violent manner). And once again, the rest, as they say, is history! The young barrister, who was thrown off a train in South Africa, rose to become the most potent force against imperialism and discrimination in India and possibly the world. The force of directed and channelised outrage against the subjugation and exploitation of man by man created a mass movement that was unprecedented in the history of British India. And finally, in 1947, under the undisputed leadership of Mohandas Karmachand Gandhi, 'the barrister who was thrown off a train', India walked into an age of freedom from foreign yoke that we all enjoy today.

These are just two examples that I have quoted. There must be many more such examples. It's not necessary that every angry man or woman should end up changing the fortunes of nations and civilizations. What is necessary is that the angry person must realise that it is human to feel such emotions and that the presence of such emotions represents an opportunity rather than a problem. So the fact that you are angry is a great opportunity. Now what you should ideally do is shut yourself up in your study and introspect. Jot the reasons of your angst. Draw a detailed battleplan. Focus yourself and your energy internally and then direct it all towards achievement of your goals. Ambition fuelled by controlled and directed anger can touch heights that ordinary ambition can't even dream of.

❐

SUCCESS STORIES : NATIONS

Having discussed the roadmap to success in the preceding chapter of this book, it is time to illustrate success with the help of some real-life examples. Success can be collective or individual. I will begin with collective success. Let us talk about some nations who have faced disaster and have come up trumps.

The United States of America

It was the year 1941. The world was in turmoil. Collective madness had struck humanity and had manifested itself in the form of World War II. While the entire Europe and Japan & China (in Asia) were battlefields, the USA was a neutral country. However, the smell of war was in the air and the breeze blowing across the Pacific was carrying it to the shores of USA. On the morning of Sunday, December 7, 1941 the entire pacific fleet of the US Navy was berthed in Pearl Harbour. Peace talks were in progress between Imperial Japan and the USA. It was in the midst of this atmosphere of hope that disaster struck. Without any warning and with overwhelming force, Japan attacked. The pacific fleet of the US, the crown of US navy, was decimated. Four powerful battleships were sunk and four others destroyed. Casualties of US armed personnel amounted to more than 2042 killed and 1282 wounded. It was a crippling and a humiliating defeat. Japan had struck where it hurt the most. Initially the entire nation was shocked and depressed. The war (for the US) appeared to be lost even before it had begun. It was in this atmosphere of despondency and defeat that the then US president Roosevelt started sculpting the features of victory. The nation went into an overdrive. Attitudes changed and before one knew it the US was on the march on the road to victory. Finally on September 2, 1945, Imperial Japan, which had won the first round convincingly surrendered unconditionally before the US and forever changed the power equations of the world. After that victory, the USA never looked back and, to date, it is the undisputed superpower of the world.

Japan

The story of Japan is even more inspiring as it is touching. It is a story of transformation from victor to vanquished and then to victor again. It is a story of exemplary courage and sacrifice for the motherland (or fatherland as the Germans would call it). After the victory in Pearl Harbour, Japan suffered massive reverses in its war against the USA. As war infrastructure ran out and aircraft carriers became scarce, it became impossible for Japan to reach the shores of the USA in order to launch an offensive on US mainland. With the battleships of US navy surrounding its shores, the Japanese put forward the greatest show of bravery and self-sacrifice seen by the world till then. *Kamikaze*-Pilots filled their planes with explosives and started crashing them on US warships. They inflicted heavy damage and alarmed the leadership in the USA to such an extent that they had to take the horrifying decision of dropping two atom bombs on Japan. On August, 6, 1945 the B-52 flying fortress christened 'Enola Gay', piloted by Paul Tibbets dropped 'little boy' on Hiroshima. The resulting mushroom cloud is still one of the starkest pictures of WWII. The dropping of 'fat man' on Nagasaki followed three days after the strike on Hiroshima. The twin strikes completely destroyed two of the most important industrial cities of Japan. The casualties were in excess of 200,000, almost all of them civilian. The industrial capacity of Japan was almost reduced to nought. After these blows, the war was over for Japan. The once Imperial military and industrial power lay humbled, humiliated and destroyed at the feet of the adversary whom it had defeated so convincingly only a few years ago. To add insult to injury, Japan was made to sign a humiliating military treaty by the US whereby it was forbidden to raise its own military in future. Instead it was to remain under the protection of the US military. Essentially, Japan was reduced to being a non-entity in post-war world. Not even the greatest visionary could have predicted the turn that Japan, as nation and economy would take. But the Japanese were and are a tough lot. They decided to put the past behind them and concentrate on the future. And concentrate they did! Soon Japan emerged as an industrial and an electronic giant, becoming an economy to reckon with. The only nation in the world to have suffered twin nuclear-bomb strikes (and that too on its heart) became renowned for the quality and technological superiority of its products. It became the leading economy of the world and its companies soon started dominating the US market. Even today Japanese companies in the electronics and automobile sectors are global market leaders and Japan is one of the most prosperous nations of the world which is admired and envied by the entire world. And mind you, they accomplished all this despite being one of the nations of the world with the poorest resources and despite being situated in one of the most tectonically active and seismically unstable regions of the world. I am not attempting to write the history of post-war Japan. I am only trying to drive home the point that if a nation and its people are committed for success, not even nuclear bombs can stop it from achieving it.

Germany

When WW II began it was Germany that was the favourite. German war machine was efficient, technologically the best, both large and deadly. The German Blitzkrieg (Lightning War) was something the world had never witnessed before. On the morning of September 1, 1939, at 4:45, German tanks left their borders and over ran adjoining Poland. Soon other small nations of Europe followed and on June 25, 1940, France surrendered. It appeared that Hitler's Germany would soon be the master of entire Europe. That Germany had achieved such a miraculous military capability only 22 years after its defeat in WW I is inspiration for any nation. Britain remained the only nation standing against the German Blitz. And stand it did! Under the exceptional leadership of Sir Winston Churchill, the then prime minister of Britain, the UK fought tooth and nail against Germany. They stood their ground long enough and with the US joining the war against the Axis powers; new strength was induced in their stand against Hitler. They often say that luck favours the brave and Britain was no exception. Hitler made the fatal mistake of attacking Russia at the wrong time. He suffered devastating reverses in Russia. Then onwards, the Allies gained rapidly. On August 25, 1944, France was freed and in April 1945, as the allied forces marched into Berlin, Adolf Hitler, the Fuehrer, committed suicide in his bunker with his wife Eva Braun, and, with that World War II was over. On October. 6, 1949 Germany was split into two parts, East and West Germany. The wall separated families and generations for forty long years till the Germans decided that enough was enough! East and West German leadership sat together honouring the decision of their citizens and on November 12, 1989 the wall separating the two nations was demolished. Today Germany is once again the richest nation of Europe renowned worldwide for the finesse and strength of its engineering.

There are other examples too like the unbelievable growth of the Asian Tiger Economies followed by an equally spectacular collapse in 1997-98. It appeared that the bubble had burst irreversibly. But the Tiger Economies bounced back and are once again on the growth graph. Similar is the story of China, a nation once humbled by the British (in the opium wars) and then by the Japanese (WW II) and perceived worldwide as a backward, agrarian economy. The same China is one of the fastest growing economies of the world on date with an annual GDP growth rate in excess of eleven per cent. Chinese products flood markets worldwide (including India) and the once backward nation is today a military, economic and sports superpower of the world.

❐

SUCCESS STORIES: PERSONALITIES

Abraham Lincoln

Abraham Lincoln, the sixteenth and arguably the best known and the most respected President of the United States of America, was born to poor parents on February 12, 1809 in Hardin County, Kentucky. His father, Thomas Lincoln was a carpenter by trade.

Soon after his birth his family was forced to shift from Kentucky to Indiana, an area which could safely be termed as 'wild'. There the family lived in a simple log-cabin with a mud floor and grew corn and vegetables for subsistence.

As a boy, Lincoln received little formal education. The aggregate formal schooling of Abraham could not be more than one year and that too came in fits and starts. As a student young Abraham had no slate so he used the ground as a slate and a stick as a pencil.

Abraham was deeply attached to and influenced by his mother who had a strong personality. However he lost even that support when his mother died on October, 5th 1818 of a mysterious epidemic christened 'milk-sickness'.

Abraham grew up to be a tall and well-built man. He supported himself by doing manual labour till the age of 21. Having received little or no formal schooling, Lincoln continued to self-educate himself and began private study of law on the strength of borrowed books. Eventually, he earned his licence to practice in 1836 and went on to become one of the best lawyers of Illinois where he had settled.

Abraham Lincoln saw a string of failures which are as follows:

- 1832 Lost job and was defeated for state legislature
- 1833 Business Failed
- 1835 Sweetheart Died
- 1836 Suffered a nervous breakdown
- 1838 Lost contest for the post of Speaker
- 1843 Failed to get nominated to Congress
- 1848 Lost Renomination to Congress
- 1849 Rejected for the post of Land Officer
- 1854 Lost contest for US Senate
- 1856 Lost contest for nomination for Vice President of USA
- 1858 Lost contest for US Senate once again
- 1860 Elected Sixteenth President of the United States of America

If this does not impress you nothing will! If someone like Abraham Lincoln can become the most celebrated president of the USA, surely becoming a doctor, engineer, sportsperson, artist, or whatever you wish to become in life is not so daunting a task after all!

Lal Bahadur Shastri

Lal Bahadur Shastri was born as Lal Bahadur Srivastava on the 2nd of October 1904 at Ramnagar in Varanasi District of the province of Uttar Pradesh. Born to poor parents his was a difficult childhood. His father Shri Sharda Prasad was a schoolteacher who later became a clerk in Allahabad. Thus he did not enjoy any of the advantages of a privileged childhood that his predecessor, the first Prime Minister of India, Pundit Jawaharlal Nehru enjoyed. A man of short stature, slight build and plain looks, he could hardly be picked as the obvious choice as successor to the charismatic and handsome Nehru.

As a young boy, Shastri had to face great hardship. Legend has it that he used to swim across the Ganges in order to be able to reach school, because he did not have enough money to pay to the boat-ferry that carried people across the river. In any case, he laboured hard to educate himself and eventually earned a doctorate from Kashi Vidyapeeth (Now Benaras Hindu University) in Varanasi.

Shastri was an active participant in the freedom struggle of India and spent a total of nine years in prison on account of his participation in the same. Following India's independence, he held important offices. He was appointed Parliamentary Secretary in his home state, Uttar Pradesh. Later he became the Minister of Police and Transport of the same state.

In 1951 Shastri was appointed the General Secretary of the All-India Congress Committee and in this capacity he directed his party to spectacular electoral success in the general Elections of 1952, 1957 and 1962.

Shastri became Member of the Indian Parliament for the first time in 1951. He was Cabinet Minister for Railways and Transport from 1951 to 1956. Exhibiting exemplary probity, he resigned from this position following the railway accident at Arivlur in Tamil Nadu, in which 144 passengers lost their lives.

In 1957, the electorate of India returned Shastri to the Parliament in the general elections. He then held the portfolio of Minister for Transport and Communications, followed by that of the Minister of Commerce and Industry. In 1961, he became Minister for Home, a portfolio which is, to-date, next only to the office of Prime Minister in its importance.

After the death of Jawaharlal Nehru on May 27, 1964, Shastri became the second Prime Minister of Independent India on June 9 of the same year. However, the trials and tribulations of Shastri were far from over. In August 1965, war broke out with Pakistan. It happened at a time when the nation was facing food shortages. However, Shastri, belying his short stature and lack of physical prowess, exhibited a steely strength of character. While overcoming the problems on the food front, he met force with force and within 22 days of the first Pakistani incursion on Indian soil, Indian forces had brought Lahore, the heart of Pakistan under artillery fire. Pakistan had suffered a decisive and humiliating military defeat and Lal Bahadur Shastri had become a national hero. The story of Lal Bahadur Shastri illustrates how the lack of money, status, background, connections, physique and beauty, all can be overcome by sheer strength of hard work, honesty and self-belief.

Thomas Alva Edison

Born on February 11, 1847 in Milan, Ohio, Thomas Alva Edison had very little formal education as a child. Like Abraham Lincoln, his total schooling was not more than a few months. However, he was a very curious child and his curiosity often led to him being branded as a nuisance. I am sure that you, like all of us, must have read the story where Edison, as a young boy, tried to hatch a chicken out of an egg by sitting on it!

At an early age of thirteen, Edison started working. His first job was that of a newsboy, selling newspapers and candy on the railway station. However, even while doing this work he continued to educate himself on science and technology and eventually gained enough proficiency in telegraphy so as to be able to land a full-time job as a telegrapher.

In 1868 Edison received his first patent for an electric vote recorder. However, this invention was a commercial failure. That, of course did not deter him and he continued his work as a freelance inventor. Just a year after his first invention (and commercial failure) Edison unveiled his second invention called the 'Universal Stock Printer'. He earned forty thousand dollars from it. From then on there was no looking back. In 1879 Edison publicly demonstrated the use of his incandescent bulb and the other systems required to make it work. This work ultimately gave rise to Edison General Electric, (Now known only as General Electric) and started the electric age.

Founding the electric age was not enough for Edison. So, from 1870 to 1890 he concentrated on founding the modern music industry. He improved his earlier invention, the tinfoil phonograph, and developed all the associated systems required to make it a commercial success.

As if this was not enough, Edison developed motion pictures in 1891 and founded the movie industry, the mother of the Hollywood and Bollywood of today!

Not satisfied, Edison embarked on his next quest of developing a modern storage battery. Eventually he developed the alkaline battery which went on to become his most profitable invention.

Apart from his lack of formal education, the story above appears to be a success story throughout. Doesn't It? Well, I agree that Edison's is a story of super success. But each of these successes was built upon a foundation of failures. Take the light bulb for instance. ***Edison failed ten thousand times*** in his experiments before he could finally demonstrate the light bulb successfully! It is a tribute to his perseverance that we have electric lighting today. Now if we take each of his experiments as a test, then he failed the test ten thousand times before he passed! And here we have young people committing suicide after failing to make the grade just once! Chew on this story about Edison. I read it on the Internet:

"In 1914 Thomas Edison's factory in West Orange, New Jersey, was virtually destroyed by fire. Although the damage exceeded $2 million, the buildings were insured for only $238,000 because they were made of concrete and were thought to be fireproof. Much of Edison's work went up in smoke and flames that December night. At the height of the fire, Edison's 24-year-old son, Charles, searched frantically for his father. He finally found him, calmly watching the fire, his face glowing in the reflection, his white hair blowing in the wind.

"My heart ached for him," said Charles. "He was 67, no longer a young man and everything was going up in flames. When he saw me, he shouted, "Charles, where's your mother?" When I told him I didn't know, he said, 'Find her. Bring her here. She will never see anything like this as long as she lives.'"

The next morning, Edison looked at the ruins and said, "There is great value in disaster. All our mistakes are burned up. Thank God we can start anew."

Three weeks after the fire, Edison managed to deliver the first phonograph."

From Growing the Distance: Timeless

J K Rowling

J K Rowling was born as Joanne Rowling to Peter James Rowling and Anne Rowling on the 31st of July 1965 in, Goloucestershire, England. Her early life was as uneventful and as average as that of any other girl of her age in England. She completed her college from France and moved back to England in order to work as a bilingual secretary for Amnesty International. Though Joanne enjoyed writing and telling fantasy stories as a young girl, it was only as late as 1990 that she started writing the first of the 'Harry Potter' Novels. In December that year Rowling's mother died. Soon thereafter, Rowling moved to Portugal and started teaching English as a foreign language. It was in Portugal that she met and married a Portugese Journalist named Jorge Arantes in 1992. The first and only child of the couple, a baby daughter, was born on 27th July, 1993.

However, things took a turn for the worse and the couple separated in November, 1993. With her mother dead, marriage finished and a baby less than a year old, Rowling moved to Scotland, and settled down in Edinborough in December, 1994. It was during this period, unemployed and living on the support of state help, that Rowling came down with Clinical Depression and even contemplated suicide! However, through all this hardship, she did not abandon the project that she had started four years earlier. Writing in cafes using an old manual typewriter, she finally finished the manuscript of her first novel, "Harry Potter and the Philosopher's Stone" in 1995. However, completing a manuscript is one thing and getting it into print is another. The manuscript of the first Harry Potter book was submitted to twelve publishing houses and was rejected by each one of them. Undeterrred, Rowling persisted and tasted first success when Editor Barry Cunningham of Bloombury publishing house in England agreed to publish the book. The first advance that Rowling got for "Harry Potter" was £1500. The rest, as they say, is history. Since then Harry Potter books have sold more than 400 million copies. The Global Brand worth of Harry Potter as a character is estimated at close to US $ 15 Billion! The last four Harry Potter titles penned by Rowling have set records as the fastest selling books in the history of publishing! Rowling's personal fortune is estimated at more than $ 1.0 billion! Numerous awards and recognitions have been showered on her and she is today recognized worldwide as an author, billionaire, celebrity and philanthropist. All this has been achieved by J K Rowling in the space of about a decade, in the face of abject poverty, heartbreak and rejection.

The story of J K Rowling goes to show what can be achieved by persistance in the face of adversity. She could easily have given up "Harry Potter" in the years from 1990 to 1995 in the face of bereavement, divorce, loss of job and mental illness. Even after 1995, she could have been overwhelmed by the initial complete rejection of her work. But she persisted. The story of J K Rowling is a living example of what faith in your abilities and work can do even when the world seems to be pittted against you.

Oprah Winfrey

Oprah Gail Winfrey was born on January 29, 1954, in rural Mississippi to an unwed teenaged couple. Her mother, Vernita Lee was a housemaid and her father Vernon Winfrey was in the armed forces at the time Oprah was born. In any case Oprah did not enjoy any formal parenting, as, as per her own version, her conception was the result of a single sexual encounter that her parents had. Her parents parted ways soon after her birth. Devoid of parental care, Oprah lived the first six years of her life in abject rural poverty with her grandmother Hattie Mae Lee. The poverty was so extreme that young Oprah wore dresses made out of potato sacks and was the object of ridicule and fun for her peers. As if this was not enough, her grandmother would often beat her if she misbehaved or refused to do her chores. The only silver lining in this phase was the fact that Oprah's grandmother taught her to read before the age of three. Aged six, Oprah moved back with her mother in Wisconsin. It was during this stay with her mother, from age six to fourteen, that Oprah went through the hell called child sexual abuse. Again, as per her own account, she was sexually molested by her cousin, uncle and a family friend from age nine onwards. Oprah became pregnant at the age of fourteen and gave birth to a son who died shortly after birth. Any one would expect that a child who had gone through so much misery and seen so much evil at such a young age would end up a bitter failure in life. But, that was not to be. At the age of fourteen, Oprah got her chance. She was sent by her mother to live with her father. Vernon was a disciplinarian and encouraged her education. Soon Oprah became an honours student at her High School. She also became a member of her high school speech team and was voted the most popular girl of the school. Her oratory skills won her scholarship to the Tennessee State University where she studied communication. During her stay at the University, Oprah won the title of 'Miss Black Tennessee'. It was also during this period that a local black radio station 'WVOL' hired her as a part time newsreader.

Winfrey moved to Chicago in 1983 in order to host a talk show on WLS-TV. It was a half-hour show with a low rating. However, within a few months of Winfrey taking over the show, it became the highest rated talk show in Chicago. It was subsequently renamed the 'Oprah Winfrey Show', was increased to one hour in duration and was broadcast nationally. Soon the Oprah Winfrey Show became the top rated day-time talk show in entire America.

Today, a woman who was born to teenaged-unwed-parents, shunted around since birth from mother to grandmother to mother to father, raped at the age of nine, forced into unwed motherhood at the age of fourteen and lost her only son soon after birth is an international celebrity, billionaire, philanthropist, book critic, media mogul, and an academy award nominated actress. She has also been assessed as being possibly the most influential woman in the world!

The story of Oprah Winfrey goes to illustrate how the complete lack of opportunity and presence of exceptional hardships can be overcome if only one concentrates on one's core strengths and is willing to grab on to any opening that presents itself. Think about it. Are your conditions anywhere near as bad as that of young Oprah?

Stephen Hawking

The story of Dr. Stephen Hawking is as touching as it is inspiring. It is a story of the victory of human will over the worst of odds. By all accounts, the life of Dr. Stephen Hawking is an inspiration for anyone who thinks that destiny has been tough on him. That is because it is the story of a man who has achieved fame, fortune and professional recognition of the highest order despite being completely paralysed!

Stephen William Hawking was born on 8th January, 1942 in Oxford, England. His father Dr. Frank Hawking was a research biologist and his mother Isobel Hawking, a political activist.

Hawking was extremely intelligent but was never rated as a brilliant student. He went on to study physics at Oxford University receiving his BA degree in 1962. Thereafter he commenced study of astronomy but soon left Oxford to join Cambridge University where he studied theoretical astronomy and cosmology. At Cambridge he started developing symptoms of the dreaded disease known as Amyotrophic Lateral Sclerosis, (ALS), which is a motor neuron disease and leads to complete paralysis of the body, eventually causing death. At that time he was only 21 years old. However, undeterred, he concentrated on his work and went on to complete his PhD. In the meanwhile, in 1965, he married Jane Wilde. After completing his PhD, Hawking became a Research Fellow and then a Professional Fellow at Gonville and Caius College. Achievements followed in quick succession and Hawking was elected as one of the youngest fellows of the Royal Society in 1974. In 1982 he was made a Commander of the British Empire. 1989 saw him becoming a Companion of Honour.

It would have been a fairytale success story, but for a little inconvenience called ALS, which had completely paralysed Hawking by 1985. In the same year, during a visit to Geneva, Hawking contracted Pneumonia and an emergency tracheotomy had to be done in order to save his life. That took away his power of speech. One of the greatest scientific geniuses of all time was now a silent vegetable in a wheelchair! However, displaying rare courage, Hawking started using a voice synthesizer (computer) in order to communicate with people.

In such a pitiable condition, when anyone else would have lost the will to live, Hawking authored A Brief History of Time. Published on 1st April, 1988, it went on to become a best seller and brought to him both public fame and fortune *(I have read the book. It is a phenomenal work and highly recommended to the lay reader interested in science, in particular, cosmology*). Black Holes and Baby Universes in 1993 and The Universe in a Nutshell in 2001 followed this book.

Today, Hawking occupies the Seat of the Lucasian Professor of Mathematics at Cambridge University. It is a chair, which has formerly been graced by personalities no less than Paul Dirac, Charles Babbage and Sir Isaac Newton! Widely regarded as the most important and influential physicist since Albert Einstein, Hawking's theories may well lead to the answer of the mystery about the origin of the Universe and the discovery of the Grand Unified Theory, the holy grail of modern physics. Coming from a person who was given only three years to live when he was 21 years old, and has been completely paralysed for more than 23 years, it is a story of exemplary courage and outstanding achievement in the face of most crippling disability.

❐

THE UGLY DUCKLING

Having read all that I have written in the previous pages, you must be wondering how I am qualified to write such a book. I mean I am successful (at least by Indian Standards). I have a secure and high-ranking government position, status and respect in the society and a loving family to boot. "What does a person like you know about adversity?" you may ask. Valid question once again. In response to this question, I think that its time I told you the story of the real Ugly Duckling, the story of the author of this book, Gaurav Krishna Bansal.

My story begins on the 28th of July, 1974 in a city called Hisar in the Indian Province called Haryana. I was the second son to be born to my parents. My father, Shri Kunwar Krishna Bansal is a 1967-batch Indian Police Service officer of the UP-cadre and my mother Dr. Mrs Veena Bansal, a social activist, a housewife and a homemaker. So, to begin with, I was born in a normal Indian family with a relatively high status in the society and was not, what you would term a 'disadvantaged' child. But advantage and disadvantage are relative terms. Monetarily, we were never very comfortable and my father was hard pressed by the extreme demands that his service made on his time and energy. I was advantaged in the sense that I went to good schools and was well fed and well clothed. But I was disadvantaged in the sense that the schools that I attended had children coming from much richer and equally (if not more) influential families. My father had humble beginnings in as much as my grandfather had expired when my father was still studying, without leaving behind any kind of inheritance for his five children that could be called 'substantial'. The salaries of government officers, though still low, were in those days, frightfully small. As a rule, any government officer, who did not have a strong family background (monetarily) was obliged to lead a rather frugal existence (presuming that he was honest). My father, I am proud to say, was and remained, an honest officer till his superannuation from service. This led to a paradox in my life rather early. I enjoyed the status of the son of high ranking police officer but never had the money in my pocket to back up that status. In those days I could only look with fascination at the new and enticing things that my classmates brought to school. From the latest and most fancy school bags, to magnetically operated stationery-boxes to expensive battery operated toys, to coveted bicycles...my classmates had them all.

My early years were spent in a school called Cathedral situated in Hazratganj, Lucknow. It was a prestigious missionary school of the city, which boasted of children of the crème-dl-la-crème of the city in its classrooms. Most of my classmates were bright and accomplished and could boast of being in possession of the objects of desire that I have mentioned above. A few of them were virtual celebrities excelling in all fields from academics to extra-curricular. In comparison to such classmates, I was a virtual non-entity. Added to that, the lack of any status symbol and even a decent bicycle, made my situation more precarious. I thought that I was deprived, short, and bad looking. I used to be extremely fond of kite flying and spent most of my spare time pursuing the hobby with a single minded dedication, seen rarely in children of my age! That, of course, meant that I had little time left for things like studies and homework. It was not as if I was a mischievous child. In fact, I was quite the opposite. I was shy and withdrawn and would remain silent in the class (usually staring at the roof) to such an extent that it prompted one of my teachers named Mrs. Emanuel to honour me with the title of 'philosopher of the class'. All attempts of my teachers at making me complete my homework failed. My more able classmates either ignored me or made fun of me. It was only natural that I developed a bit of an inferiority complex and became even more withdrawn.

I remember an incident that was particularly bad for my self-confidence. I was in class eight when one of my classmates, Saurabh Sharma, decided to form a bicycle club. Saurabh was an excellent student and was always one of the three contending for the top spot in the class, the other two being Aseem Agarwal and Roop Kumar Bhadury. Aseem was in all ways an exceptional student and it was a normal feature for him to score one hundred per cent marks in subjects like maths and science. He was also a participant in extra-curricular activities and was the blue-eyed-boy of the teachers. He, however, was hyper-competitive in his approach. Roop, on the other hand was almost as good as Aseem in his academics and the difference between him and the former was typically one mark here or there. But, all-round, Roop was definitely the best student of the class, and arguably, of the entire school. He had a pleasant personality, excellent command over the English language, was a wonderful singer and an actor par-excellence. Saurabh was likewise a whiz at studies and not so bad either in extra-curricular activity. Together, the trio were enough to give a complex to any other student. I perhaps was no exception. So when the idea of the bicycle club came up, I dearly wanted to be a part of it. However, not having a bike of my own, I was flatly refused the membership. I can still remember the disappointment and the sense of deprivation I felt. I naturally linked the rejection with my looks and lack of academic excellence. This perception was heightened by the fact that Aseem, Roop and Saurabh were all in the club.

It was unfortunate, but in our class, there was an atmosphere of extreme competitiveness among the ones running for the top slot. Saurabh and Aseem were the leaders in this competition business. Roop was into it, but not to the extent that would make him unpleasant. However, it was a common feature of the first ten in the class, excepting me. Despite my lack of interest in academic pursuits, by some kind of magic, I always remained in the first ten of the class. So to that extent, I could also not be termed as a bad student. In those days, the dearest wish and perhaps the only wish of my father was that I should stand first in my class. Perhaps if I concentrated on my studies the way my other, more accomplished classmates did, I could have achieved this goal. But the problem was that somehow, it was never a goal for me. It was this lack of competitive spirit and inclination to enjoy my kite flying that set me apart from my classmates and prevented me from mixing with them. The icing on the cake was that I was more interested in 'girlish' activities like growing plants and keeping pets than 'gentlemanly' activities like cricket and other sports. So the net result was that I had practically no friends in my class till I reached the seventh standard. In such a situation I used to vent my feelings by writing and composing poetry. That was also a well-kept secret and my poems were mostly written in one notebook that was kept securely locked away in my little closet at home. So, in the ultimate analysis, I was lost in my own world and had little perception of the competitive atmosphere in the class. Life continued in this manner, till a decision was taken to shift me Cathedral to Mahanager Boys' Inter College due to reasons that I cannot write as they may be damaging to the reputations of some of my ex-classmate and faculty (at Cathedral).

Mahanagar Boy's was and still is one of the best schools of Lucknow and I was lucky to have scored enough marks in the final exam of class eight so as to be able to secure admission there. But, fate was not yet ready to smile on the ugly duckling.

I was admitted to class nine in Mahanagar Boy's. As I have mentioned before, I was shy and withdrawn. The effects of the disastrous experience that I had during the last year had further added to my lack of self-confidence. In such a circumstance, having been separated from the only two friends I had, namely Roop and Namita, I was easy prey for bad company. And that is precisely what happened. I do not exactly recollect what I did in that fateful year, but one thing I do recollect is what I did not do. And the singular thing that I did not do was study! When the results of the final exam were out, my name figured in the very small list of failures. I had secured five out of hundred in maths and ten out of hundred in science! The same boy who had always been one of the first ten in the class till a year back was now the only boy to fail in his class. To top it all the school decided to rusticate me and my name was deleted from the list of students. When my father came to know of this state of affairs he was distraught. I still remember his words, "Son I am ashamed of you". My father met the principal of the school, Brother Mani, who decided in his kindness to readmit me on the condition that I would have to repeat the class. With that failure, I became a virtual untouchable. Students and parents reading this story will understand the status of a boy who fails in his class, among his peers and their parents alike. So it was no surprise that all my friends except Roop and Namita abandoned me. I will never forget one line that both of them said to me on different occasions. I quote "Gaurav, you are not like that, it has just happened to you". This single sentence gave me a lot of strength and I decided to sit down and take stock of my situation. After much thought I came to two conclusions: one, I would not repeat class nine, and two, I would do all that was in my power to avoid repeating class nine. As was customary at that time, a failed student was given a promoted certificate if he decided to leave the school. I decided to quit Mahanagar Boy's and was given a promoted certificate. Then once again the humiliation started. I approached Cathedral for a readmission but was flatly refused. Then I tried Colvin Taluqdars College, where my elder brother was a respected student. Colvin also denied admission to me. It was at that point of time that I decided that I would do my plus-two from Colvin Taluqdars only. But the main issue remained unresolved. From where and how was I supposed to do my high school (class ten) when no school was willing to give admission to me. It was in such trying circumstances that a glimmer of hope appeared. A government school called Agrasen Inter College, agreed to admit me to class ten on the basis of the 'promoted' certificate. It was, by all means a modest place though certainly nothing when compared to the schools I had gone to earlier. Moreover the medium of education there was vernacular (Hindi) while I had studied with English as the medium of instruction all my life. It was a culture shock for me. But I decided to grin and bear it.

I still remember my first day at Agrasen Inter College.

I reached the school on time all decked up in my brand new uniform. In this school the children came from much humbler backgrounds than mine and that reflected in their general appearance. So it was no surprise that I shone forth as a new pin in my spic uniform. With a spring in my step I reached my new classroom. It was nothing compared to the classrooms that I had occupied. The desks were dilapidated and the benches were in various stages of obsolescence and decay. The windows were just wide open gaps in the wall without shutters or panes. But it was a classroom all the same and it was class ten! I had achieved the little goal that I had set for myself. I was not going to repeat class nine after all. Just as I reached my class, I found a strange looking boy standing there. He was tall and thin with a clean shaven head and was wearing something which looked like a uniform.

While in Mahanagar Boy's, I had developed a very foul language. I would use cuss words at the drop of a hat. I used such language almost as a status symbol! So, once again, it was no surprise that I used the same fowl language to greet the strange character standing in front of me. Imagine my surprise when, listening to my language, that boy did not flinch at all. Instead he looked straight into my eyes and said a single sentence which changed my way of talking for ever. He said, "achche ghar ke lagte ho. Tumhaare muh se ye shabd shobha nahi dete" (You appear to belong to a good family. Such language from you does not behove your background). I stood rooted to the spot gaping for words. It was almost as if God himself had admonished me using that boy as a medium. In an instant I could see the morass that I had fallen into. Coming from such a distinguished family I was using the language used by the filthiest and most undesirable characters. I apologised instantly. That boy introduced himself as Prasanna Kumar Nigam. (Later we became good friends). From that day onwards I simply gave up that manner of speaking. I can't even ***begin*** to tell you the kind of change it brought into me. Just giving up the use of such language straightened my thinking process. Soon I befriended other students of my class and started working hard on my maths and science, the two subjects in which I had failed in class nine.

It was in Agrasen Inter College that I started

participating actively in extra-curricular activities. The school was a little known government institution and was never invited to the bigger competitions that used to be organized by other, more famous, institutions from time to time. In the year 1990, when I was a student of class ten at Agrasen, my school received an invitation for a debate competition after a long hiatus. It was a small, low profile, competition that was being organized by the Jain community of the city. The first prize was one hundred rupees (roughly US $2.5). It was a handsome amount for a student in those days. I read the notice and decided to participate. The only problem was that I had ZERO experience of public speaking. Previously, only once had I attempted to go on stage and give a speech. It was in an inter-house debate competition that had been organized in Cathedral when I was there in class eight. I still remember the experience. I was the first speaker to be called on stage, something for which I was not mentally prepared. In any case, I went on stage and immediately became a terminal case of stage fright. My knees started shaking uncontrollably, my mouth went dry and my tongue felt as if it was made of sandpaper. Try as I would, no words came out, and I just stood there gaping like a fish out of water. After what seemed like an eternity (though only a few minutes had elapsed), I was able to mutter a strangled "thank you" and climbed down from the stage. My exit was greeted by a full round of applause, only that it was the kind of applause that is designed to humiliate and not praise. I felt so miserable that I excused myself to the washroom and remained there till I could get the opportunity to slip away from the hall to my classroom.

With this kind of a background in public speaking, it was indeed a bold and ambitious decision to participate in a debate. Nevertheless, I went to the teacher in-charge of cultural affairs in the college and requested him to allow me to participate. The teacher in question, Shri D P Mishra was one of the senior most teachers of the school. His subject was Hindi. Slightly bald, with a fair complexion and a steely gaze, he was quite an intimidating figure. However, he was fond of children and dearly believed that the school must do well in cultural and extra-curricular activities also if it had to earn a name for itself. However, his previous experience and effort in this direction had not yielded much fruit. This was primarily because of the lack of participation from the students in the events for which the school did receive invitations. So when I went and told him that I had read the notice about the debate, on the notice board, he just asked me one question. And that question was whether I was serious about participation and whether or not I intended to get cold feet and back out at the last moment. I told him that I was indeed serious about the whole issue and also that my previous experience of public speaking was NIL! To that his reply was that if I was serious and committed, previous experience was of no consequence. He asked me to prepare a draft for or against the motion (as I wished) and to show it to him the next day. The debate was in Hindi and the topic was "Bharat Ki Akhandta Bas Ahinsa Se Hi Sambhav Hai" (The integrity of India as a nation can be ensured only by non-violence). Since the debate was being organized by the Jain community, which is a stickler for non-violence, it was best to speak for the motion and support the assertion that only a Gandhian policy of Non-Violence could ensure long term integrity of the nation. I, however, felt otherwise. So I decided to speak against the motion. I prepared a draft and took it to Guruji the next day. To my delight and surprise, he praised what I had written and suggested a few alterations that I promptly made to my draft. Then followed rounds of rigorous practice personally monitored by Guruji. He made me speak in front of him, then in front of the class, and finally in front of a fully convened assembly of the entire school. Soon the shaking knees disappeared and the dry mouth felt normal again. I found that I was speaking confidently and clearly. I doubled my practice and soon the d-day came. It was with a mixed feeling of apprehension and confidence that I climbed the stairs of the stage that day. "What if I suddenly forgot all that I had so painstakingly prepared and rehearsed? What if the microphone decided to conk out at that very moment? What if I was booed off the stage even before I began? But I had prepared well and that episode in Cathedral two years ago was history. I should be able to pull this one off." Such were the thoughts running helter-skelter in my mind during that short walk to the stage. A numbing nervousness started to creep in and the much-dreaded weakness in the knees started appearing. The saliva in the mouth started drying up like a little puddle does in the harsh sun after a brief shower of rain. And the tongue started to acquire a most-unpleasant raspy texture. There was a strange tightness in the abdomen and tingling at the tip of my fingers. I felt as if the whole world was sitting there with the express purpose of ensuring that I fail. I felt like turning around and running away. It was with such thoughts that I took the microphone in my hands. Then, before beginning to speak, I took a look around the hall. I found that there was a look of expectation rather than hostility on the faces of the audience and the judges alike. That look told me that they were not sitting there with the purpose of trashing me ab-initio but were expecting me to perform. I then took a deep breath. That further steadied my nerves and I began to calm down. The symptoms of nervousness began to disappear. Finally I pictured my last practice session in the school when I had spoken before a full-convened assembly. The number of students and teachers there had certainly been more than the number of people in the audience here. I felt a surge of confidence and began my speech. Words flowed and expressions emerged. Before I knew it the allotted five minutes were over and the entire hall erupted in applause. A brief, stolen glance, at the judges told me that I had done well as there were smiles and looks of approval on their faces. The competition went on and finally it was time for the result. The chairman of the session announced the prizes. Third prize was announced first. My name did not figure. Then came the second prize. My name still did not appear. Finally it was the turn of the first prize winner. "And the name is.." there was a brief pause, "Gaurav Krishna Bansal". I could not believe my ears. I had won the first prize! A look at Guruji was enough to reduce everything else to miniscule proportions. He was beaming. He walked up to me and placed an affectionate hand on my head as I touched his feet. Back in school it was celebration time. It was after a very long time that the school had won a first prize in *any* competition. From then on, invitations for various events started coming to our school. Under the able guidance of Guruji we formed a formidable team, which participated in activities as diverse as public speaking to dramatics to singing. That year the school lifted more trophies than ever before and our team became well known and respected for its prowess in the schools of Lucknow. Personally, for me, it was a year of transformation. I became the star of the institution. Love, praise and respect from peers and superiors alike came to me in a manner I had never experienced before. I developed a command over Hindi and became a confident public speaker. The hunger to succeed started burning within me. I concentrated harder at my studies particularly on the subjects that had let me down in class nine. ***More than anything else I realized that my previous failure was mostly due to my own shortcomings.*** In the class ten exams (board exams as they are called in India), I did well and scored seventy three per cent marks in aggregate with honours in all subjects save one. The triumph was, of course, in Maths and Science. Just one year ago, my scores in these subjects were five per cent and ten per cent respectively. And now, just one year later, in an open exam, I had taken my performance up to seventy nine per cent in Maths and eighty one per cent in Science! With my mark sheet, I walked into the admissions office of Colvin Taluqdar's College. Without as much as a hiccup I was admitted and given my chosen combination of subjects. The second goal stood achieved. I had promised myself that I would secure admission in this very college, which had refused to admit me one year ago. The promise was fulfilled. The ugly duckling was beginning to grow some new feathers.

Getting admission is one thing and making a success out of it quite the other. When I entered Colvin, I was on a high. I was a star student from Agrasen Inter College. But here things were different. Once again I was in the company of students as or more accomplished than me. But this time, they were willing to befriend me also. Soon I had a group of friends and time started passing away merrily. Before I knew it, the final exams of class twelve (intermediate final-year) were in sight. But something was wrong. I was just not prepared for the exams. Desperately I tried to catch up but it was an uphill battle. I managed to pass and secure sixty two per cent marks in aggregate but I had fallen full eleven per cent marks below my aggregate percentage in class ten. Moreover, I had not participated in any other activity worth mentioning. But still I was happy. I had after all secured marks in excess of sixty per cent (which is termed first-class in Indian System). However, once more the honeymoon was over. It was testing time once again. I was a student of life sciences and was aiming to become a doctor. Of course, this aim was not so much mine as of my parents. But I did not have any objection to it. Having studied life sciences in school, it appeared to be the natural choice to make. Now the next step was competing in and qualifying the pre-medical entrance examination (PMT). This is a competitive exam conducted at the province and All-India level and the students securing a place in the merit-list are allotted medical colleges based on their choice and their place in the combined merit list. As was customary or rather fashionable at that time, I decided to 'drop' a year and join a coaching institute in order to prepare for this competitive exam. By 'dropping a year' it is meant that the year after I passed out of Colvin Taluqdar's College, I did not join any undergraduate course (B.Sc./BA/ B.Com etc) in any university. It was a bad decision and my parents were vehemently against it. Even my teachers and other well wishers cautioned me against such a move. But I refused to listen and decided to risk the year that I had fought so hard to save after my failure in class nine. It was not as if the move was entirely baseless. The underlying presumption was that a student who dropped a year for preparation could, in theory, devote all his time to the task at hand and make a success out of it in the first attempt itself. But practice is often quite different from theory. I joined a reputable coaching institute of Lucknow. However, once there, I fell in bad company once again. My friends, I have no reservations in admitting, were a set of boys devoid of any vision, ambition or purpose. They were all wasters who came from rich backgrounds and had joined the coaching institute more with the intention of coming in touch with girls and having fun rather than with the intention of successfully competing in PMT. A few capable friends whom I had in Colvin became engrossed in their own studies. The result of such an approach (or lack of it) and lifestyle was obvious. The results of the PMT were a complete disaster for me. I had failed to make the grade in all the exams that I took. It was once again back to the drawing board for me. I sat down and did an analysis of my strengths and weaknesses. For the first time I gave a serious thought to whether I really wanted to become a doctor in the first place. I realized that it was a goal set by others rather than by myself. I found that actually becoming a doctor was not what I wanted to do. I must stress that at that point of time, I was yet not clear as to what I did want to do. It was just that I was sure that I did not want to become a doctor. Even then, it was a big jump. At least taking the decision of not becoming a doctor (albeit in the negative sense), prevented me from sinking another valuable academic year in the pursuit of something that I did not want to do! So this time around I appeared for competitive entrance exam to the University of Lucknow and succeeded. I was also allotted my chosen combination of subjects, viz Zoology, Botany and Chemistry.

The University of Lucknow, or 'Lucknow University' as it is more popularly known is a heady place. I will not say that it is the best University in this world or even that it is among one of the best Universities in the world. In fact, globally the institution (perhaps) has no ranking. It is, however, a very old University and has produced a President of India (Dr. Shankar Dayal Sharma), apart from a plethora of alumni who have distinguished themselves in all fields of scholarship. As it usually happens, any place with a long history tends to be a mixture of sorts. It's a bit like a very old field that has healthy crops and old established weeds in the same measure. So it was up to the student who joined this university to decide whether or not he wanted to excel as a scholar. Let me be candid and admit that there were innumerable opportunities available for doing every thing that was non-scholarly in nature. I for one, having given up my intention of becoming a doctor, decided to concentrate on my studies. I decided that I would abstain from selective study and guess papers and would try to cover my entire course for the year and also gain a command over my subjects. Easier said than done. It was once again an uphill climb. Passing the final exam was not an issue. In fact, the way the system worked, it was easy to pass the exams by doing just selective study and relying on guess-papers. However, I was trying to master my subjects. And that, let me add was rather a tough preposition. The course was huge and demanded intensive study. So I decided that I would set aside a certain time every day just for study and would make it a point to study ***every day.*** This was one resolution I stuck to. Soon I started to make rapid progress and began to be rated as a good student by my teachers. I also revived my hobby of public speaking and started to participate in the numerous events (debates, declamations, extempore etc) that were organized by various departments of the University from time to time. Soon I became known as a formidable speaker in my University. It was at this point that chance intervened and I was invited to become a part of a cultural troupe comprising of students from different departments of the University. The troupe was called 'Sansarg'. 'Sansarg' is a Hindi word, which translates into 'Coming Together' in English. Ours was a motley group. We had singers, dancers, choreographers, and even fashion models! Through this group, I had a chance to step out of Lucknow and participate in cultural festivals organised by Harcourt Butler Institute of Technology, Kanpur (Odyssey), Indian Institute of Technology Kanpur (Antaraagni), Banaras Hindu University (Spandan) and an All India Level Debate in Jawaharlal Lal Nehru

University, New Delhi. It was an eye-opening, horizon-broadening experience. I won laurels in public speaking, and dramatics. Soon I developed the ability to speak extempore, in chaste Hindi and English, on any subject under the sun. Side by side my grades were showing an improvement year after year. By the time I completed my graduation, I was back to my percentage in high school (73%). At the same time I had collected so many trophies won in various competitions that there was no place in the house to display them. Graduation over, it was decision time once again.

Once again, I did a SWOT analysis. I found that I was good at language and expression and had advanced quite a bit in the direction of gaining a command over the life sciences. I also found that I had the ability to study independently and regularly. I realized that these strengths were required to clear the Indian Civil Services Exam.

The ICS exam is a three stage selection process comprising of a Preliminary Exam, A Main Exam and a Personality Test (interview). Any candidate aspiring to be a Civil Servant in India has to appear in and clear all the three stages of this competition. It is a gruelling, one year long, process and a candidate of general category (to which I belong) is allowed only three attempts to achieve the same. Appearance in the preliminary test is counted as an attempt. The exam is made even more competitive by the fact that 50% of the available seats are kept reserved for Scheduled Castes, Scheduled Tribes and Other Backward Castes as per statute. So, essentially, for a general caste candidate, the competition becomes twice as fierce as the number of available vacancies is reduced to half. Further, for me, the decision to appear in this exam right after doing B.Sc. was akin to a team like Hong Kong aspiring to win the cricket world cup! As a student, I was a minnow in a sea populated by Sharks. I knew that in this arena, I would be up against the best brains in the country, Engineers, Doctors, Management Professionals, Chartered Accountants, PhD Scholars...the list of backgrounds of the participants in this competition was as formidable as it was intimidating. But a decision is a decision. So I decided to stick to it. However I was careful not to repeat the mistake of dropping one year as I had done earlier. So I appeared in the Competitive Entrance Exam for securing admission in the Department of Management, Lucknow University (popularly known as LUMBA-an acronym for Lucknow University Master of Business Administration). I was confident that I would qualify in this exam, but the result was a real whopper. I had topped! It was like an intravenous dose of confidence. Before I knew it, the date for the Civil Services Preliminary exam came. I can vividly recall that experience.

I occupied my chair in the examination hall. I felt nervous. It was for the first time that I was appearing in an exam of this stature and prestige. Soon the question papers were distributed. It was the first paper of the optional subject (zoology in my case). This paper has 120 multiple-choice-type questions, which have to be solved in 120 minutes.

At the signal of the invigilator, I opened the seal of the cover and began answering the questions. To my horror, I found that I was not sure about the answers to the questions on the first two pages. My spirits plummeted. Two pages translated into more than ten questions. In an exam, where every question counted, not knowing the answers to ten questions was like losing the battle without firing a single shot. But good sense prevailed. Instead of wasting time on the questions that I did not know, I moved ahead. On the third page, I got my first shot. It was a simple, straightforward question and I could have answered it in my sleep! The first black circle on the OMR sheet (answer sheet) sent a wave of thrill inside me. I answered rapidly, circling and leaving all the questions that I did not know, or was unsure about for later. Soon, in about 60 minutes, I had completed my first round of the question paper. Once again I began from the first page. By this time the butterflies in the stomach had gone to sleep and the hand was less shaky. To my surprise and delight, I discovered that I had not been able to answer the questions on the first two pages due to my nervousness. Actually, most of them were simple questions phrased in such a manner that they appeared difficult. Soon the time was up, and I had completed the paper. I reckoned that I had answered around 85 out of 120 questions correctly (including intelligent guesses which were allowed in the exam at that time). It was not a bad performance, though it could not be considered a very good one also. However, I was happy. I had performed much better than I initially thought that I would. The next paper was the compulsory paper of General Studies. This paper has 150 multiple choice type questions, which have to be answered in 120 minutes. It is considered a particularly daunting paper because it is not subject-specific and contains questions from fields as diverse as history to mathematics and

Geography to Current Affairs. This time, there were no butterflies in the stomach. I opened the seal and started answering the questions, adopting the same approach that I had adopted in the first paper of Zoology. I answered well and my estimate at the end of the allotted time was that I had answered around 85 out of 150 questions correctly in this paper also. The performance was good for a first timer, but not good enough to make a candidate sure of clearing the first round. But it was futile to think about the round that was over. So I began preparations for the main exam, the second round.

The main exam in the ICS competition is totally subjective and is of 2000 marks. There are seven credit papers; two of general studies (300 marks each), four of optional subjects (300 marks each) and one of essay (200 marks). Added to this were two non-credit, but qualifying, papers of Vernacular and English. I really put my nose to the grindstone this time. I do not recall how much labour I put in. Suffice it to say, that it was as hard work as any human being could put in. It was with a spring in my step and confidence in my heart that I started answering the first paper of this leg. The exam passed without incident and I thought that I had done well. Soon the result came. And what a result it was!

In those days, there was hardly any Internet penetration in India. Results were declared through newspapers. There is an office of Press Information Bureau in Lucknow. The result of the main exam was wired to this office at around midnight from where it was sent to all the major newspapers of the city to be published in the edition of the next day. On that fateful night I reached the PIB office at half past midnight. It was chaos! The result was pasted on a wall and hopeful candidates were practically climbing over each other in order to locate their number in the hallowed sheet of paper. Some how I managed to reach the wall and set about finding my roll number. I did not remember what my roll number was, but I did remember that the last digit was '8'. The dot-matrix printer used to print the sheet was obviously good as the roll numbers were clearly visible. Frantically I searched for my roll number. Finally, I came to one roll number in which all the digits were the same save the last one. The last digit in that number was '0'. "It must be a misprint", I thought. Again and again I looked at that zero expecting a faint black horizontal line to appear and turn it into an eight. But that did not happen. The zero remained a zero. The reality struck home like a punch in the abdomen. I had failed to clear the second stage of the exam! After the euphoria of clearing the first stage and the blood, sweat and grime of the following three months, it was back to square one again.

It was the first time in my life that I had worked so hard for anything. It was only human that after clearing the first round of the exam and doing well in the second round (in my own estimation) I was expecting to reach the third round. The unexpected crash was, therefore, extremely painful and demoralizing. The place was full of students who had failed to qualify for the personality test. For each successful candidate, there were three who had failed to make the grade. The scene was heartbreaking. There were candidates who had exhausted their attempts. There were others who were at the end of their tether. Tear stained faces, bowed heads and smashed dreams populated the verandah of the Press Information Bureau. Amidst such an atmosphere, one could be forgiven for thinking that it was impossible to succeed in this exam. For a little while even I started thinking on such lines. Then I turned around and saw a tea stall in front of the PIB office that was open at that hour. I also noticed that a few candidates who had cleared the main exam were standing there sipping tea and laughing and joking amongst themselves, hardly giving a glance or a thought to the pandemonium that was going on in the verandah of PIB. Instinctively I felt like being a part of that small group of successful people rather than the crowd of unsuccessful candidates I was standing with.

At the tea stall, I sat on a stool sipping tea and listening to and watching the small group that I have just mentioned. They were young men just like me. You could not have looked at anyone of them and guessed that these were men who were on the verge of becoming senior officers in the Government of India. Soon they left, but I kept on sitting there lost in my thoughts. I pictured myself at the time I had begun preparing for the exam. At that point of time, I was a part of approximately three hundred thousand hopefuls. After having cleared the preliminary test, I had left behind approximately Two Hundred and Ninety Five Thousand candidates! No small feat I thought. Merely by clearing the prelims, I had become one among the five thousand candidates, from being one among more than quarter of a million. True, not clearing the mains was a debacle but still, my performance till now showed that I had a decent chance of clearing it in the next attempt. This thought immediately lifted my spirits. Quickly I finished my tea and drove back home.

Within a few days the mark sheet arrived. To my astonishment, I found that I had scored very poor marks in my optional subjects (Zoology and Botany). It was unbelievable. These subjects were my bread and butter. For the world of me, I could not fathom where I had gone wrong. I decided to do some research on the issue. The following morning, I went out and bought and issue of a competition-oriented magazine that had published the interviews of the top rank holders of the previous years. In that magazine, there was the interview of a lady officer who had secured a rank among the top ten and had done it with the same combination of subjects as mine. In her interview, she had also given a list of books that she had studied from. That list was an eye opener. I had not even heard the names of the authors of majority of the books that were listed. I immediately rushed to my bookseller and asked him to get me all the titles in the list. He had some of them available with him. The first book he produced was on Genetics (By Gardner). One look at the volume told me what had gone wrong with my preparation. I had simply not read the correct books! The books that I had used in my preparation were useful for an undergraduate. But this was a different league altogether. I knew that I had to bring about some serious changes in my home library. This brought another issue to the fore. The books were prohibitively expensive. So I adopted a dual approach. I bought a few which covered almost all the topics that I was required to read. For the rest, I approached my University lecturers. They were kind enough to provide me access to the Departmental libraries where I was able to locate almost all the books that I required as per that list. Not only that I was also able to get hold of some additional titles which could be used for value-addition to my preparation. My teachers got the books issued for me and soon my library was bustling with the kind of armament I needed to win the battle in my second attempt. With renewed vigour, I started my preparation for the second attempt at the Civil Services Exam.

While all this was happening, I was pursuing my management degree side by side. It was a double whammy for me. MBA is not an easy course. The subjects relating to the humanities were not so difficult but there were others like mathematics, statistics and accounting, which made life much tougher. The only way out was to integrate my studies for an MBA degree with my preparation for the Civil Services Exam. I figured that I could use much of the material from my MBA course to enrich my base for the General Studies paper. I was weak in maths and statistics and the general studies paper contained a section of fifty marks comprising of just these two subjects. So, by working hard on my problem areas in MBA, I was also increasing my chances of scoring well in the Civil Services exam.

Time flies, they say. And in my case it flew jet-powered. I was halfway through my second and final year of MBA when I appeared in the prelims for the second time. This time I had the confidence of having cleared this stage once more, and I solved my papers quite confidently. Immediately afterward, an analysis at home told me that I had done well and was almost certain to make it through this stage for the second time in a row. The result confirmed my intuition. Now it was time to take on the mother of all exams, the main exam.

My second main exam went off well. I was confident of a positive result this time round. Before long the result was declared and sure enough, this time I was a part of the little group sipping tea and laughing and chatting at the tea stall in front of the Press Information Bureau. The feeling was heady. I was within sniffing distance of the dream. Just one test remained between me, and the hallowed portals of the Indian Civil Services. And this was the test I was least worried about. It was the personality test-or the 'interview' as it is more popularly known. I had not faced a lot of interviews before, but had always performed very well in the ones I had actually appeared for. This time I was playing on home turf.

In the blinking of an eyelid it was 24th of April 1999. I got down from the car of my uncle at the Gate of the Union Public Service Commission at New Delhi. The journey this far had been momentous. The minnow in the sea of scholarly sharks had grown big. The Ugly Duckling was almost fully fledged.

The interview was gruelling, probing and extremely challenging. It was like nothing I had ever faced before. A panel of five experts of high stature and scholarship quizzed me. They asked questions from fields as diverse as the Sufi tradition in India to the issue of the global scarcity of fresh water. I was forthright, honest and confident in my replies. The attitude of the members of the board was supportive and pleasant but I was aware that they were dissecting my personality and looking for any obvious flaws. The interview lasted approximately forty-five minutes. After the interview, there was nothing more to do but wait.

In the meanwhile, MBA second year was coming to a close. I busied myself with preparations for the final exams. That also gave me a much-needed relief from result-anxiety and the time passed easily.

It is the practice that the names of the top rankers in the Civil Services Exam make front-page news every year. It was the month of May and the final result was expected any day. For two or three nights, I visited the PIB office consecutively only to be told that the result had not yet been declared. Then I missed a night.

The next morning, I picked up the newspaper habitually and saw the photograph of the first position holder of the Civil Services Competition on the first page. That photograph was not mine. With a beating heart, I turned the page. On the next page was the complete list of successful candidates with their names arranged in decreasing order of rank. My name was not there in the first ten. It was not there in the first fifty. It was not there in the first hundred either. Soon the truth dawned. My name just wasn't there...! I couldn't believe it. It was catastrophic! How could it happen to me two times in a row? And this time I had committed a cardinal mistake of not preparing for my third attempt. This was partly due to my overconfidence and partly because I was too busy preparing for my final semester exams of MBA. In any case, I had no option but to skip the Civil Services Exam of 1999.

1999 passed without much incident, save a broken wrist of the right hand. It was a scooter accident and the fracture was bad. With my right hand out of action, I could not have written the main exam that year. So, on hindsight, it was just as well that I did not take an attempt that year. But, all the same, I must stress that I missed that year not because I had received some divine warning about the expected fracture in October, but because I had failed to prepare for the prelims that year. So, in the ultimate analysis, it was a dead loss.

As before, I analysed my mark sheet. I found that I had done reasonably well in my personality test, securing 190 marks out of 300. However, my debacle was due to the fact that I had scored low in the written exam and, as a corollary, had missed a place in the merit list because of a low aggregate (written and interview combined). What was even more shocking was that once again my optional subjects had let me down. No doubt, my performance had improved in all the subjects, but it had not improved in proportion to the work and resources that I had put in. So once again, it was back to the drawing board for me.

This time, I understood that there was some fundamental flaw in my answers that was preventing me from getting good marks. So I consulted my professors in the university. From them I received a few valuable suggestions. First: Attempt those questions, which have sub-questions (parts). Second: While answering questions on life sciences, have a diagram oriented approach rather than descriptive. Third: Bring out the structural functional linkage clearly when attempting questions in Zoology and Botany. And Fourth: Understand the question before trying to answer it. "Just four suggestions?" you may say. But here lies the importance of guidance. Actually, just one right suggestion is enough to change the result in your favour if you follow it earnestly. And I was lucky enough to get four! Needless to say, I reoriented myself and started practicing on the new lines.

I took the third attempt at the Civil Services in the year 2000. Since I had had a sabbatical of one full year, I was very well prepared. By now the preliminary exam had become almost a non-issue for me. However, this year I decided to appear in three exams, namely: Indian Civil Services, Indian Forest Services, and Uttar Pradesh Provincial Civil Services. The course content was the same in all these exams. The Indian Forest Service exam did not have a preliminary stage and was open only to science graduates. The service was however at par with other services allotted through the Indian Civil Services Exam. I wrote the IFS exam in July 2000 and the other two exams in September and October-November 2000 respectively. I got interview calls for all three after the written exam. I could write reams about those interviews and I am sure that it would make interesting reading. But suffice it to say, that this time round I faced the panels with more maturity and less anxiety. I had exhausted three attempts of Civil Services and one of IFS (there is no attempt limit for PCS). Now one attempt of Civil Services and two of IFS remained.

I do not remember the date, but clearly recall all that happened that night. It was past midnight and I had gone off to sleep when our domestic help (who lives with us) came rushing to my room. He woke me up and announced "Bhaiyya aap officer ban gaye, papa aapko upar bula rahe hain" (Brother you have become an officer. Dad is calling you upstairs). I was about to give him a ticking off for waking me up from my sleep when his words practically exploded in my ears. If dad was calling me then it had to be true. I rushed upstairs to find a beaming father. He told me that the father of one of the candidates with whom I had appeared in the same interview panel for IFS had called and informed him that his daughter and I, both had been selected and that I had secured fourth rank in the country! It was phenomenal! In any competition of All-India stature, securing a position in the first ten is considered to be a sterling achievement. And here was I, the minnow, with the fourth position under my belt. But the news needed to be confirmed before we could celebrate. So I drove off to the office of PIB. As usual, an impersonal piece of paper was pasted there with the names of the candidates successful in the IFS exam written on in descending order of rank. And this time, I did not have to wish for any horizontal or vertical line to appear on the paper. My name was there on the fourth position in bold black letters. The struggle was over. I was finally a class-one officer of the Government of India. The Ugly Duckling was staring in the lake and looking at his own reflection.

The results of Civil Services and Provincial Civil Services followed in quick succession. I was selected in both. After that it was celebration time. In one stroke detractors were silenced. I had the satisfaction of having reached where I had decided to reach. The road had not been easy. It was a process of taking myself to another level of scholarship. There were times when I felt confused, and depressed. Often the obstacles seemed to be insurmountable. There were heartbreaks on the way. Ties with some people whom I had valued as friends snapped under the strain. However, enduring bonds were formed with others, which continue to-date. There were times when I felt like giving up. But it was precisely at such occasions that I told myself that I had made a decision. I was committed and I had to fulfil my commitment at any cost. My efforts had to be honest and I had to transform all my potential into performance in the direction of achievement of my goal. Failure was not an option and all available opportunities had to be utilized. If an attempt was there to be taken, it was to be taken. While there is no denying the fact that at times the journey was traumatic, on the whole it was enriching. In my eyes, I began as the ugly duckling. However, there came a day when I looked at my own reflection and I saw a swan.

I do not say that what I achieved was the pinnacle or epitome of achievement. In fact, by all accounts it was a modest achievement. But there is no denying that achievement it was! Of course, there are others who have achieved much more in the same time when compared to me. Take Sachin Tendulkar for instance. He is only one year elder to me and has achieved fame and fortune beyond anybody's imagination. Compared to him, my feats appear insignificant. But the success and achievement I have been talking about is personal in nature. Remember, at the very outset I defined 'success' as a 'decision'. You are successful when you reach where you had decided to reach. It is not a game of comparatives. Rather it is a game of absolutes. Often we make the mistake of benchmarking our success against the standards set by others. This is a big mistake. Success is a very personal phenomenon. It is more about reaching personal goals, than otherwise. Take for instance a farmer who decides to raise a crop, which is ten per cent more than the previous year's and does. To me that farmer is just as successful as the entrepreneur who decides to make a million dollars in five years and does. The question is not so much of the goal per se as it is of the goal-achievement match. So long as the set target is achieved, success is ensured. To that extent there are no degrees of success. It is not a variable quantity. It is a constant. To the extent the desired goal is achieved, success is ensured, otherwise not. The magnitude of the goal does not matter. In fact, in order to ensure success it is essential that the goal set for one's self should be achievable. By 'achievable' I mean 'possible'. True, Napoleon said that the word 'impossible' exists in the dictionary of fools. And I tend to agree with him. Truly speaking nothing is impossible in this world. It is only a matter of time and effort before an apparent impossibility is brought in the realm of the possible by human endeavour. And that is precisely why I have used the term 'achievable'. Achievability of a target means the possibility of meeting the target given finite time and resources. As individuals the time and resources at the command of each one of us are limited. Given unlimited time and resources, everything is achievable. But the finiteness of these two attributes puts certain things out of the grasp of an average human. So it is futile, even counterproductive, to set targets that do not fit into the realm of achievability. Allow me to illustrate. Suppose an aspiring author was to set a target for himself. What would be the achievable target? It could be getting published by a reputable publisher or winning the Nobel

Prize with the first book. I think that all of us will unanimously agree that the former is achievable and the latter is not. I would say that the former is immediately achievable so it should be the immediate goal. The latter is not outside the realm of achievability but it is sufficiently unachievable so as to be classified as a long-term possibility. An author who follows the path of first setting a target of getting published has every chance of meeting his target and becoming successful. But an author who aims for the goal of winning the Nobel Prize with his first published work is only befooling himself. So, it is essential to have a long-term vision and break it down into short-term goals. If you are planning to become an author, by all means go ahead and set the target of winning the Nobel Prize. But after you have done that concentrate on the immediate goal of producing a work that would be accepted by a well-respected publisher. Once you get published your self-image and self-perception will improve. You will not see yourself as a failure but as a success. The achievement of the short-term goal will inspire and motivate you to work harder towards your ultimate objective. And that is where the story of the Ugly Duckling becomes relevant. The story, mind you, is not so much about how the world perceives you but about how you perceive yourself. A negative self-image is the mother of all failures. Setting unrealistic goals only takes you towards greater failures and ensures that your negative self-perception is reinforced. On the other hand, achievement of small goals breaks down the same and enhances your self-esteem and self-image. Once you develop the confidence and attitude of an achiever, no goal is too big for you.

Look at the whole phenomenon of success as a staircase with infinite steps. The moment you scale one step it becomes the home base for scaling the next one. In essence, the moment you achieve one target, it becomes a thing of the past and a new target beckons you. Nothing much changes except that as you move higher, your self-perception goes on improving. As you continue to climb, your desire to achieve becomes stronger and your efforts in that direction more concrete. You may never go ahead and proclaim to the world that you have indeed become a beautiful swan but internally you will feel that indeed you have metamorphosed. The admiring glances of the people around you will echo your belief.

And that is what this book is about. It is about self-belief. Self-belief is the bedrock of all motivation and all success. So if you really feel that you are the proverbial Ugly Duckling sit back and take a good look at yourself. Who knows there might be a beautiful swan inside you waiting to come out and look at its own reflection in the water of the lake.